COLLECTED POEMS

Books by Lucien Stryk

Taproot
The Trespasser
Zen: Poems, Prayers, Sermons, Anecdotes, Interviews
Notes for a Guidebook
Heartland: Poets of the Midwest
World of the Buddha: An Introduction to Buddhist Literature
The Pit and Other Poems
Afterimages: Zen Poems of Shinkichi Takahashi
Twelve Death Poems of the Chinese Zen Masters
Zen Poems of China and Japan: The Crane's Bill
Awakening
Heartland II: Poets of the Midwest
Three Zen Poems
Selected Poems
Haiku of the Japanese Masters
The Duckweed Way: Haiku of Issa
The Penguin Book of Zen Poetry
The Duckpond
Prairie Voices: Poets of Illinois
Zen Poems
Encounter with Zen: Writings on Poetry and Zen
Triumph of the Sparrow: Zen Poems of Shinkichi Takahashi
Cherries
Bird of Time: Haiku of Basho
Willows
On Love and Barley: Haiku of Basho
Collected Poems 1953–1983

COLLECTED POEMS

1953-1983

Lucien Stryk

SWALLOW PRESS

ATHENS OHIO □ CHICAGO □ LONDON

Swallow Press books
are published by
Ohio University Press
Athens Ohio 45701

Library of Congress Cataloging in Publication Data

Stryk, Lucien
Collected Poems 1953-1983

I. Title.
PS3569.T76.A6   1984   811'.54   84-2583
ISBN 0-8040-0855-8
ISBN 0-8040-0856-6 (pbk.)

For My Mother, My Father
and Leonora

CONTENTS

From *The Pit and Other Poems* (1969)

From *Afterimages: Zen Poems of Shinkichi Takahashi* (1970)

Awakening (1973)

From *Selected Poems* (1976)

New Poems (1983)

NOTE

This gathering of three decades contains but a handful of pieces, some revised, from my first books, the Fantasy Press (Oxford, England) collections *Taproot* (1953) and *The Trespasser* (1956). The poems from *Afterimages: Zen Poems of Shinkichi Takahashi* (Swallow Press, 1970), were translated with the assistance of the late Takashi Ikemoto. The poems from my other Swallow Press volumes, *Notes for a Guidebook* (1965), *The Pit and Other Poems* (1969), *Awakening* (1973) and *Selected Poems* (1976), appear, mainly, in their original order.

Work on some of the new poems, in the last section, was made possible by a Rockefeller Foundation Fellowship and was partially supported by an Artist's Grant from the Illinois Arts Council, a state agency. For permission to use new poems, I thank the editors and publishers of the following: *American Poetry Review, Bonniers Litterara Magasin* (Sweden), *Calliope, Celebration, Chariton Review, Chicago Sun-Times, Confrontation, The Georgia Review, The Nation, New Letters, Northwest Review, Poetry* ("Cherries," copyright 1978, and "November," copyright 1982, Modern Poetry Association), *Poetry Now* (BBC Radio 3, London), *Quarterly/West, Raccoon II, Shearsman* (Malaysia), *The Small Towner, TriQuarterly, The Poet's Choice,* edited by George Murphy, Tendril Press, Green Harbor, Mass., 1980, *Willows,* Embers Handpress, Cambridge, England, 1983, and *Cherries,* Ampersand Press, Roger Williams College, Bristol, R.I., 1983.

LUCIEN STRYK

Mind, mind, mind—above the Path.
Here on my mountain, gray hair down,
I cherish bamboo sprouts, brush carefully
By pine twigs. Burning incense,
I open a book: mist over flagstones.
Rolling the blind, I contemplate:
Moon in the pond. Of my old friends,
How many know the Way?

—Zengetsu

Part I

From *Taproot* (1953)
and *The Trespasser* (1956)

FARMER

Seasons waiting the miracle,
dawn after dawn framing
the landscape in his eyes:

bound tight as wheat, packed
hard as dirt. Made shrewd
by soil and weather, through

the channel of his bones
shift ways of animals,
their matings twist his dreams.

While night-fields quicken,
shadows slanting right, then left
across the moonlit furrows,

he shelters in the farmhouse
merged with trees, a skin of wood,
as much the earth's as his.

SOUTHERN TALE

From deep in the town the dancers' stomp
Will not rouse him now,
Where he hangs like a cracked bell:
Dark engulfs the man, the ashen cross.

The girl steps back and dreams—
O he the night and she the slippery moon,
And high the cotton flew!
It was like swimming in the river,
Water pressing to her deeps,
Ropes the arms that pulled her down,
The river banging on the wharf.

She looks away, her whiteness
Blending with the moon,
And hears the flies
Maddened by the smell of horse,
The smell of flesh.

From deep in the town the dancers' stomp
Will not rouse him now:
The arms, tongue,
Giant thighs are mute.

MASK

Behind the tattered brow
    the skull looms sharp:
as branch survives its fruits
    and wind-picked bark,
so bone releases flesh
    to weather nakedly
and lone: on winter's frost
    burns summer's day.

SCARECROW

Battered hat set firmly,
arms flapping lazily,
scarecrow's futile grimace
invites the passing crow
to feast on all the greens
a scraggy plot can grow.

Shaped by frost and sunburn,
termite and hen,
coat shreds reeking,
trousers billowing,
his windy eyes commend
beaks that snap and rend.

Long humiliation
turns him stiff and sour—
as the whole of Crowdom
from out the speckled air
feeds on rows of cabbages,
pods of plumping peas.

THE STACK AMONG THE RUINS

The tangled brush and bombed-out fields reflect
And blur into the sky; harsh thunder
Rings the image to the raging sea. War
Reels again to staring eyes, where thoughts collect
In webs of fear—stirring musty brains
And hearts—then shudder through the victim veins.

No smoke lifts from the broken chimney's lip
Where winds hurl down to jar the blistered fields:
It stands alone, a maniac that yields
No breath or word, but raddled by the dip
And twist of day, turns inward to a grief
That's like an arm shaped through an empty sleeve.

There stands no more than stone on broken stone,
Yet memories converge to form a shaft of pain,—
Bruising the inner eye, scarring the brain;
Then spreading on the ruins the rusty sun
Frees the tortured mind with blasts of fire,
Flashes on the chimney stack and sags the worn barbed wire.

THE ACROBAT

Hands reach out to grasp the dipping rope
Which weaves an awful silence on the watching
Horde below. Taller than the crows that ring,
Their shadows shearing, through the leafless oak
The acrobat draws closer to the looping hands;
While, lifting from those fatal arms, his eye
Seeks images that swarm across the sky,
Then fall through boughs to merge with twisting strands.

The air grows tense within the bracing bow of day.
The hands are raised to snap the dancing cord.

Words that sought his tongue remain unsaid—
Torn in his throat. Above, the branches sway
Against the wind's astonished flank. The horde
Draws back from where his hugeness dangles dead.

CHU MING-HOW

Chu Ming-How, the Mandarin,
Astride his fat brown mule,
Rode slowly up a high green hill
To dodge the lowland din,
   The tassel on the mule's long tail
   Swished gaily in the sun.

Half-way up the mule sat down
And drowsy Chu fell back,
Removed his shoes and dusty pack
And dozed upon the ground,
   The scarlet button on his cloak
   Cast scarlet all around.

But still into his wise old head
The lowland troubles crept
So on the mule's moist rump he leapt
And flogged his way ahead,
    The cherries on the hill were grouped
    In patterns white and red.

Then under a dripping cherry tree
He unrolled his silk and pen
And while the mule brayed down the sun
He sketched the rose-blue sky,
    Which wore a tasseled button
    Above the shading tree.

Part II

Notes for a Guidebook (1965)

THE BEACHCOMBER

Beyond the patchwork bobbing of her back
The nineteen peaks of Sado float
In violet mist. Below, the "Exiles' Route"
Is taut with sail and net. Across
The humps of sand that blot the sea
The pinetrees hold the beaten shore,
And just as she is wasted by a cold
Necessity, the iced Siberian wind
Has bent and shriveled to their salty core.

She dreams a raft of treasure to her reach:
A silky foam will wash ten lacquered bowls
Like frozen blossoms to the beach,
And she will pluck them with a girlish hand.
Now as the sunset, like a vulgar fan,
Spreads slowly on the exiled peaks
She scoops and hurls a pebble at the waves.
But nothing happens. From those crystal founts
The frail and scattered richness never breaks.

HEARN IN MATSUE

That all was miniature gave him comfort
    Of a sort,
And after the Lady, Ellen Freeman,

To whom he had written finally, "Do not
    Disgust me,
Please—" the women were so otherworldly

It was like a permanent exhibition
    For which one
Scarcely had to be the connoisseur. In fact

He shut his eyes and took the nearest for both
  Bed and name
(He had tired of his); was bowed into a house

Which brushed the river a crane's cry from the
  Daimyo's Tower;
Started fussing with the garden; pushed his wife's

Few things around the room like chessmen; until,
  Pleased at last,
He braced for winter which, though wet, was very

Beautifying. He was often seen tramping from
  The bathhouse,
Flesh a-tingle, all rose against the snow.

Came time to work: a cub again, he snuffed for
  News in Old
Japan, and, stiff on haunches, englished along

With a nameless one or two, tales which drew
  The expert's
Touch like lacquered puzzle-boxes and, when solved,

Would gush from prospects charged with mountains
  Called Giraffes,
Trees tense as wire, a moon which always snared

In pineboughs, and temples which could pull one
  To the knees.
The fame did not surprise: it had awaited

Him like those fragrant ports of forty
  Years ago
The tall black hulls of home. It fit him, and he

Wore it as he felt, deservingly. What as
  Years crept by
He would not learn to bear, and ill deserved,

9

Was wife, friends, job, food, the too familiar
        Land itself,
And now, in winter, the Siberian wind

That tore across the sea to heap him at
        The brazier
For months, weak eyes pricked by dying charcoal.

It was then, remembering Shelley and his
        Fading coal,
He knew how much he hated all Romance.

RETURN TO HIROSHIMA

I. *Bombardier*

Coming out of the station he expected
To bump into the cripple who had clomped,
Bright pencils trailing, across his dreams

For fifteen years. Before setting out
He was ready to offer both his legs,
His arms, his sleepless eyes. But it seemed

There was no need: it looked a healthy town,
The people gay, the new streets dancing
In the famous light. Even the War Museum

With its photos of the blast, the well-mapped
Rubble, the strips of blackened skin,
Moved one momentarily. After all,

From the window one could watch picnickers
Plying chopsticks as before, the children
Bombing carp with rice-balls. Finding not

What he had feared, he went home cured at last.
Yet minutes after getting back in bed
A wood leg started clomping, a thousand

Eyes leapt wild, and once again he hurtled
Down a road paved white with flesh. On waking
He knew he had gone too late to the wrong

Town, and that until his own legs numbed
And eyes went dim with age, somewhere
A fire would burn that no slow tears could quench.

II. *Pilot*

All right, let them play with it,
Let them feel all hot and righteous,
Permit them the savage joy of

Deploring my inhumanity,
And above all let them bury
Those hundred thousands once again:

I too have counted the corpses,

And say this: if Captain X
Has been martyred by the poets,
Does that mean I have to weep

Over his "moments of madness"?
If he dropped the bomb, and he did,
If I should sympathize, and I do

(I too have counted the corpses),

Has anyone created a plaint
For those who shot from that red sun
Of Nineteen Forty-One? Or

Tried to rouse just one of those
Thousand Jonahs sprawled across
The iron-whale bed of Saipan Bay?

I too have counted the corpses.

And you, Tom Staines, who got it
Huddled in "Sweet Lucy" at my side,
I still count yours, regretting

You did not last to taste the
Exultation of learning that
"Perhaps nine out of ten of us"

(I too have counted the corpses)

Would not end up as fertilizer
For next spring's rice crop. I'm no
Schoolboy, but give me a pencil

And a battlefield, and I'll make you
A formula: take one away
From one, and you've got bloody nothing.

I too have counted the corpses.

III. *Survivors*

Of the survivors there was only one
That spoke, but he spoke as if whatever
Life there was hung on his telling all.

And he told all. Of the three who stayed,
Hands gripped like children in a ring, eyes
Floating in the space his wall had filled,

Of the three who stayed on till the end,
One leapt from the only rooftop that
Remained, the second stands gibbering

At a phantom wall, and it's feared the last,
The writer who had taken notes, will
Never write another word. He told all.

THE MINE: YAMAGUCHI

It is not hell one thinks of, however dark,
These look more weary than tormented.
One would expect, down there, a smell more human,
A noise more agonized than that raised
By cars shunted, emptied, brimmed again.

Today, remembering, the black heaps themselves
(On which conveyors drop, chip by chip,
What aeons vised and morselled to lay
A straw of light across the page)
Do not force infernal images.

After weeks of trying to forget,
The eye resists, the vision begged and gotten
Is the heart's: rows of women bent over
Feed-belts circling like blood, pickhammers
Biting at the clods that trundle by,

Raw hands flinging waste through scuttles gaped behind
While, a stone's-throw down the company road,
A smokestack grits the air with substance one
Might sniff below, or anywhere. It marks
The crematory, they pass it twice a day.

THE REVOLUTIONARY

Who was it said that men to forge beyond
Must jell into a mob composed of as
Many minds, fused singly, as it has heads?

A monster-maker with a taste for blood,
He would have lumped the lot and had us
Leaping impassables, breaching impregnables.

Four hundred years before the birth of Christ,
Mencius, advisor to the King of Ch'i,
Saw man as such, and in a scarlet notebook

Laid at his liege's feet, had planted characters
So rich of seed, so thick with hate of all
That eye surveyed, the tribe of lackey scholars

Gathered by the princes to find fault,
Each weighted with a royal scythe and bearing,
In wormy fist, the straw of abuse all life's-blood

Had been spent for, fell panting across the sage's tomb.
The Chinese are a thorough, hardy race,
But the Court was overstocked with geldings,

And who, however formidable,
Could have held back those squat black ships,
Crammed to the sails with early-harvest grain,

From plying westward, port to hungry port?

MOHARRAM

(Islam: month of mourning)

Where we ate in the canyon
The stream reflected, on the crags,
A hundred wavering heads
And the sun falling laced
The water with their blood.
When the sheep grazed down
To clatter round our fire
They wore those heads again,
And the stream had cleansed
The blood from every throat.

Yet none could feel at ease
As, catching our breath, we watched
The shepherd yelp them past
Gorged with the darkened grass.
By that afternoon of Tassua,
Stretched in a great arc of thirst,
The mourners of Hoseyn had flecked
The cragstones with their salt—
Tears, gigantic, rolled down to swell
The trickle misnamed stream.

The water was unfit to drink
And it burned the fingers where
The spits had turned in unbelievers'
Hands. When the sun went down
The sheep, dragging their puffy
Dugs, cropped past again to fold.
Tomorrow was Ashura, day
Of human sacrifice, not sheep's,
And blood would spatter round the gate
Of Imam Reza's Shrine.

Though safely distant, already
We could hear from the city fading
At our backs the cry of "Ya Hoseyn!"

And as on a thousand tambours
Borne as one the rough palms of mourners
Slapped against stripped chests. We bound
The spits, still smelling of our feast,
With wire, and leaving the canyon
To the dark, filed slowly down
The path those jaws had cleared.

THE WOMAN WHO LIVED IN A CRATE

She was very famous: three times she'd sailed
    The world around
In books of photographs, pressed against the
    Imam Reza's Shrine.

Summers she would squat inside the crate,
    Cracked almsbowl up,
Ten *rials* a snapshot, jaw clenched miserably
    For an extra five.

Then as the tourist scuttled off, out poked
    Veiled head, and she
Would crawl onto the sodden road to
    Spit the money clean

And gossip with the roadsweep's mule. Guiltily
    We bore her scraps
Until we saw it was ourselves, trapped in
    Thick-walled crate, we might

Have pitied: no-one picked shamed way through
    Steaming mule-turds
To fill a leaky almsbowl, while we sat
    Tittering in the sun.

A PIPE OF OPIUM

When I dropped to the floor
And Jahangir my friend,
Squatting above me, stuffed

The pellets in and lit them,
Enjoining me to puff,
His family started giggling.

At first euphoria of sorts,
Then a quick dissolving: Jahangir
And all his portly brood

Became an undertaker, seven-voiced,
Many fingered, and for an age
I stalked the purgatory

Of his atrocious living room,
Watching the Kerman carpet's
Garden wilt around me,

Feeling the Farsi cackle
Boom against the skull. I rose
Headachy and wiser. There are

Many ways to dodge reality,
Hundreds of states preferable
To the kind of life we own,

But the only satisfactory death
Takes us clean-lunged, clear-headed,
And very much alone.

A PERSIAN SUITE

I. *Delgusha Garden*

The bulbuls do not sing here
    Anymore,
And the streambeds, dammed with silt,

Do not rise to lap the
    Scented toes
Of lovers dawdling under

Aspens with Khayyam. Am I
    Alone in
Liking it this way? It was

All too much, too much, smelling
    Of Genghis
Khan and Tamerlane. Whoever

Flung those gates apart and shoved
    A horde of
Muddy beggars through to foul

The footpaths, dip sour rags
    Into the
Pond, deserves our thanks. Now

The pond's an ossuary.
    The beggars
Do not come here anymore.

And rocking the aspens, hid
    By leaves, crows
Rain droppings, and fly on.

II. *Beggars*

Like distressed ships they founder
    In ocean
That has never ceased to batter,

However calm the instruments
    Pronounce it,
Their arms like broken spars

Stretched for the saving pittance.
    Though the day
Be windless their rags blow wild,

And oh their mouths send out such
    Piteous
Signals, forever more the food

Must turn to garbage on the
    Painted dish.
They cry, but the fog is thick

And full of plunging monsters
    And the firm
Ships sailing by cannot shift

A sole degree from a course
    As rigid
As the Table of the Laws,

Those bent coins boiling in the wake
    Would scarcely
Fill the stomach of a gull.

III. *Oasis*

Nothing stands so green.
These few trees hold back
    A tide of sand

And ride the grit-blast,
Or moving with the sun,
    Which all day long

Nibbles at the grass-edge,
Twist like dervishes in
    The pool below.

Imam Reza, from all
Sides your pilgrim trails
    Stretch parched as tongues,

And chanting your name,
Balanced between water
    And death, they come.

IV.   *The Dome*

All gold, the pilgrims heap
Like coals beneath your
    Radiance.

Forever set, the wheeling
Sun must envy you. How
    Bright you burn!

Only the prophet, brooding
In the dark, knows you for
    What you are:

Bauble of Allah, how
Many sinners have purchased
    Peace with you?

V.   *Desert Song*

Shall we strike the tent now,
    And move on
Beneath the terrible sun?

We are searchers together,
    You and I,
For that the world thinks madness.

Well, let them call it so!
    What can they
Know, those bitter ones who

Wallow on the seven shores,
    Of the sweet
Rush of water to the

Aching throat? Or how dream
    The wonder
Of need beyond fulfillment?

Enough! Again I have found
    Oasis
In the cool streams of your arms.

VI. *Muezzin*

It is a matter no longer of finding
    The most durable voice:
There are records of the best, and loudspeakers

Perch like parrots in the muezzin's cage
    Atop the minaret.
So one is not greatly stirred, being

American and here for only a year,
    By all the business
Around the Imam Reza's Shrine. Yet

Walking absurdly about at always
    Brilliant noon, one can be
Hurled to the shadows when, mincing past

The beggars at the gate, black from top
    To toe, veil bulged bonily
Over nose, eyes which see but cannot,

By God, be seen plunged to the unclean heart,
    Comes woman to her prayer.
Then let all those parrots croak together,

One's still in Persia, a thousand years ago.

A SHEAF FOR CHICAGO

*Something queer and terrifying about Chicago: one of the
strange "centres" of the earth . . .*
             —D. H. Lawrence to Harriet Monroe

I. *Proem*

Always when we speak of you, we call you
Human. You are not. Nor are you any
Of the things we say: queer, terrifying.

It is the tightness of the mind that would
Confine you. No more strange than Paris
Is gay, you exist by your own laws,

Which to the millions that call you theirs,
Suffice, serve the old gargantuan needs.
Heaped as if just risen—streaming, unsmirched—

From seethings far below, you accept all.
By land, air, sea they come, certain to find
You home. For those you've once possessed, there's no

Escaping: always revealed in small
Particulars—a bar, a corner—you
Reappear complete. Even as I address

You, seeing your vastness in alleyways
And lots that fester Woodlawn, I have
A sense of islands all around, made one

By sea—that feeds and spoils yet is a thing
Apart. You are that sea. And home: have
Stamped me yours for keeps, will claim me when,

Last chances spent, I wrap it up for good.
You are three million things, and each is true.
But always home. More so and more deeply

Than the sum of antheaps we have made of
You, reenter every night to dream you
Something stone can never be. And met

However far away, two that call you
Home, feel beyond the reach of words to tell
Like brothers who must never part again.

II.   *A Child in the City*

In a vacant lot behind a body shop
I rooted for your heart, O city,
The truth that was a hambone in your slop.

Your revelations came as thick as bees,
With stings as smarting, wings as loud,
And I recall those towering summer days

We gathered fenders, axles, blasted hoods
To build Cockaigne and Never-never Land,
Then beat for dragons in the oily weeds.

That cindered lot and twisted auto mound,
That realm to be defended with the blood,
Became, as New Year swung around,

A scene of holocaust, where pile on pile
Of Christmas trees would char the heavens
And robe us demon-wild and genie-tall

To swirl the hell of 63rd Place,
Our curses whirring by your roofs,
Our hooves a-clatter on your face.

III. *The Balloon*

(To Auguste Piccard, his day at Soldier Field)

As you readied the balloon, tugging
At the ropes, I grabbed my father's hand.
Around us in stone tiers the others

Began to hold their breath. I watched my
Father mostly, thinking him very
Brave for toying with his pipe. Then when

You filled the giant sack with heated
Air and, waving, climbed into the
Gondola with a bunch of roses

Thrust at you, I freed my hand, cheered
And started clapping. I caught your eye,
You smiled, then left the ground. The people

Filed for exits when, twisting in
The wind, you veered above the lake, a
Pin against a thundercloud. But I

Refused to budge. My father stooped to
Beat me and cracked his precious briar
On the stone. And still I wouldn't leave.

He called me a young fool and dragged me,
Bawling, to the streetcar. But I couldn't
Stop watching you. I stayed up all that night,

Soaring ever higher on your star,
Through tunneled clouds and air so blue
I saw blue spots for hours. In the morning

My father laughed and said you came back down.
I didn't believe him then, and never will.
I told him I was glad he broke his pipe.

IV. *The Beach*

Even the lake repulses:
I watch them where, shellacked
        And steaming

In barbaric light, they
Huddle in their shame, the maids
        And busboys.

Even the lovers dare not
Step where the goddess rose in
        Tinted foam,

But paw each other, gape,
Spin radio dials. And hulking
        Over cards

Mothers whip strings of
Curse like lariats, jerking
        The children

From the shore when, suddenly
Across the beach, they hear:
        "Lost! Child lost!"

None rise. The breakers drown
Voices, radios; peak white, pound
        In like fists.

V.   *Mestrovic's Indians*

(Equestrian statues, Michigan Avenue)

With bare heels sharp as spurs
They kick the bronze flanks of
        The horses.

But what sane beast would brave
A river wild as this, choked
        As it is

With jagged tin and all
That snarling rubber? and
        Ford to where?

Along the other bank, while the
Great arms pointing with their
        Manes convulse

In anger, the merchants
Dangle strings of gewgaws
        In the sun.

But no mere hoof was meant
For plunging here, and why, the
        Horses seem

To ask, would even redskins
Climb a shore where not one
        Grassblade springs?

VI. *City of the Wind*

All night long the lake-blast
        Rattled bones of
Dreamers in that place of glass.

Awake, they heard a roaring
        Down the lots and
Alleyways where wind flung

Rainspout, fencepost, toolshed,
        As if the town
Were tossing on the flood

Of space. All night, it seemed,
        A horde of giants
Came trampling overhead,

Tore limbs, wrenched screens, spilled
        Glass like chips of
Sky. Next day through, the dazed

Ones rooted in the mire,
        Then, back in beds,
Dreamt the city fairer

Than before. But how,
        Snapped antennae
Pulling roofs askew,

Autos tipped hub-deep in silt,
        Could dream raise up
What dream alone had built?

VII. *Eve*

In Calcutta I found her in a stall,
        A thing for sale,
Breasts like burnished gourds: some things one does not buy.

In Isfahan her eyes were black as wells
            Entreating alms
Of all who passed: there are deserving charities.

In Amsterdam above a darkened street
            A bay window
Framed her sundries, proffering bliss: I was not sold.

In Seville she wore a gypsy shawl and
            Bangles on her
Dancing feet: the silver dropped around them was not mine.

In Paris she hugged me down the avenue,
            Skirt a jocund
Sail, towed by the dollars in my purse: I tacked for home.

In Chicago she waits behind a door
            No common key
Can budge: who enters there will never get away.

VIII. *The Gang*

One can hardly extricate them
From the props they lounge against,
Or see them for the smoke lips

Link in chains that will not hold.
At night the sound of pennies tossed
Upon the sidewalk-cracks is like

A slowly breaking mirror
Which reflects the little that they
Are. What girl dare pass and not

Be whistled at? Their appraisements
Are quick, absolute: that water
Freezes into ice needs scant

Deliberation. Whatever
The day sweeps up, their sole
Antagonist is boredom, which

By merely standing around, they
Thwart at every turn but one.
They scorn whom others envy,

The man who ambles by, duty
Snapping at the heels, and should lovers
Cross, there is a sudden flinging down

(By eyes so starved, they almost moan)
And then a coupling in the dust.
Allow them such years to lean

And wait. Soon they must approach
The selfsame corner, and hail
The gang that is no longer there.

IX.   *The Neighborhood*

Long away, I find it pure
Exotic; no matter that they roll
The sidewalks up at ten and boys

Want height to leap for basketballs:
It is a place, and there are corners
Where one does what one would do.

Come back, I find the expected
Changes: shabby streets grown shabbier,
The mob all scattered, old girl friends

Losing more of what's been lost,
The supermarts turned up like sows
To give the brood of grunters suck,

And Mother, like a thickening tree
Whose roots work deeper as the woodsman
Nears, spread over all, the wind which sweeps

Across her whispering "Stay on."
Two weeks of that, and there are
Other whispers that I heed.

The train pulls in and I descend,
To mount before it pulls away.
Goodby, Mother, goodby! I'm off

Again to Someplace Else, where
Chafing together once a month
The strangers sit and write sweet letters home.

NOTES FOR A GUIDEBOOK

In celestial Padua
The ghosts walk hugely
In the public squares.

Donatello is one,
His horseman in the
Piazza San Antonio
Guards the gruff saint's heart
Like a mystic ruby,
The ears of the horse,
Of the rider,
Riddled by prayer.

Giotto, Dante are others,
The painter's frescoes
Float like clouds
Above the city,
The poet's cantos
Ring upon its walls.

30

And what of us,
Who stand with heads
Strained back, feet tapping?
Shall we eat, sleep,
Be men again?
Shall we slip back
To the whores of Venice?—
Dwarfs, clods, motes of dust
In the brightness.

THE FOUNTAIN OF AMMANATI

(Piazza della Signoria, Florence)

Below the pigeon-spotted seagod
The mermen pinch the mermaids,
And you shopgirls eat your food.

No sneak-vialed aphrodisiac
Can do—for me, for you—what
Mermen pinching mermaids in a whack

Of sunlit water can. And do.
These water-eaten shoulders and these thighs
Shall glisten though your gills go blue.

These bones will never clatter in the breath.
My dears, before your dust swirls either up
Or down—confess: this world is richly wet.

And consider: there is a plashless world
Outside this stream-bright square
Where girls like you lie curled

And languishing for love like mine.
And you were such as they
Until ten sputtering jets began

To run their ticklish waters down your
Spine. Munch on, my loves, you are but
Sun-bleached maidens in a world too poor

To tap the heart-wells that would flow,
And flow. You are true signorine
Of that square where none can go

And then return. Where dusty mermen
Parch across a strand of sails and spars,
And dream of foamy thighs that churn.

TORERO

Some see him dancer,
Delight as the banderillas
Hit and quiver from his practiced hand,
Fall like a savage
Bird, piece by piece, talons piercing.
Yet there are those
Who cheer him as compassionate butcher,
Sniff the wild flesh on the hospital table,
Marvel as sharp ribs expand, hunger
Fades from the eyes of widows and orphans.

Others see him priest,
Pray as he sights along the sword,
Hosanna as he plunges toward the altar,
See the swordhilt as
Chalice spilling hot as flame, take the host
Of the ears, the tail,
While he circles the arena
And is pelted by hats, fans, a hundred
Twisted flowers. As the dead bull
Is dragged along the sand, these cross themselves.

And there are some
Who see great panniers choked
With easy pesetas, their gambler hearts
Choking with love
As he kneels before the bull, spreads glistering arms:
Only the torero,
Sad face stiff with fear, sees the bull.
Beyond the shrines in cheap hotels, the heaped pesetas,
The villa by the sea—horns
Like a fist of knives brush him in the dark.

IN A SPANISH GARDEN

Aranjuez, he remembered waking—
Jardin de la Isla. He lay
All night among the trampled roses
And high above him now
The one-armed faun, features haggard
In the dewy light, stared down
Like a conqueror. Somewhere
At his back a fountain dripped.

He sat up dazed and, groping round,
Snatched and shook the bottle
Like a club. The goatboy did not budge,
The fountain kept on dripping,
The scent of roses was as sour
As puke. And as he moved up
To the hedge, those little mouths
Were snapping at his heels.

Straddling the hedge, he whooped and toppled
Headlong to the path when, popping
From a lilac bush, he saw a pitchfork
Then a beard. Such screams pierced
All around him, the very leaves
Screwed up to buds again. And then

33

It was he heard the pounding of
A thousand hoofs upon wet gravel.

He scrambled up the ornamental gate
And, rocking there, watched until
He thought him blind the pitchforks flashing
At his feet like waves. He whooped again
And kicked his heels into the bars
Like bronco ribs. And then he cried—
Your bloody roses! *Caramba!*
If this is Eden, where the hell is God?

THE ROAD FROM DELPHI

The twin prophetic streams still running through
Our heads, we drank above the gorge and watched
The eagles. You remembered, as sunset
Forged a halo over you and stained
The clear wine red, the country's tragedy.
Too much history, I said, erodes the best of lands.

Yet passing Thebes again, this time in darkness,
You spoke of Oedipus, his darkness,
And now the rattling of the bus became
The work of furies. I smiled knowingly
But envied the cunning of your sex
Which makes of the flintiest peak a roost in time.

ESCALE

One remembers a port where boats
    Tap fitfully
Against wharf-poles and wharf-side shops,

Patched awnings taut, are cool as
　　　Sunlit fathoms.
At times the rooftops of the town

Swim like brilliant shoals the washed
　　　And briny air.
One remembers a bar where fish-soup's

On all hours and sailors wait the
　　　Windfall virgins
Of long sea-rocked nights. There, on a

Shimmered terrace, steeped in acrid
　　　Afternoons, they
Lean across the tables, burning,

To watch years slip like freighters
　　　Down the seaways.
And there remain, knowing the worst

Of inland days, the rot, the sloth,
　　　The ennui, to
Tramp in dream the unmarked shore.

CHEKHOV IN NICE

I

Along the Boulevard des Anglais
Tourists mistook him for Lautrec,
Though he was taller
And when not hunched over hacking
His walk was straight enough.

Perhaps it was the way he stared
At women, like a beggar
At a banquet window, and then

He was always scrabbling for a notebook
While the snickering revelers

Flowed like water round a stone.
Oh they all knew him artist.
All, that is, except the people
He would talk to in his
Scant atrocious French: the waiter,

The cabdriver, the man who
Brought his boots back in the morning
Like an oblation to Apollo.
To them he was a munificent
White Russian, title snatched,

A parcel of serfs languishing
For his return. Certainly
He was unhappy. And the chambermaids
Were touched by nailmarks
Through the blood-flecks on his sheet.

The century had just turned over,
And the Côte was never gayer.
Even the dowagers, strapped
To beachchairs all along the shore,
Felt young again and very beautiful.

And rather scornful, he was quick
To see, of the old-young man
Who moved among them like a noctambule,
His back to Mother Russia,
Seagulls screaming at his ears.

II

He had just turned forty, and now
At times he felt himself regretting.
Oh they had expected far too much

Of one as sick and poor, hung with
Unmarried sisters and a widowed dam.

Wasn't it enough to have planted
The usual imaginary garden?
Must he also, like some poet,
Sing upon the ruddy boughs?
Were he less the son, he'd have come

Here twenty years ago. Before those
Germs, swarming, had carved
A kingdom of his chest, before
The flame had risen from his bowels
To fan within his head. Were he less the son. . . .

And the reputation, so harshly won,
Did precious little good in France.
Who'd risk displeasing one who'd make of her,
However high her beauty,
A thing of pity in some dismal tale?

Foutu! he muttered as he slunk
Back to his room and tossed his hat
Upon the pile of doodled papers
On the desk. Now he longed for home.
In the few years left to him

Would come—was bound to come—
Another thirty stories and a dozen plays.
Then no doubt they'd prop his bones
Between those giants in Novo-Devechy.
But were there any choice to make, he'd act

The part of one the world was still applauding,
That country squire of his,
Petulant, bored, pining for the Côte d'Azur,
And—if one could believe those Russian hacks—
Likely to live forever.

WORDS ON A WINDY DAY

Airing out the clothes,
    The odor of mothballs
        Driving me inside,
I watch in wonder
    As the wind fills
        Trouserlegs and sweaters,

Whips them light and dark.
    In that frayed coat
        I courted her a year,
In that old jacket
    Married her, then brushed
        Her tears off with a sleeve.

The wind blows through them,
    Tosses them about,
        These mildewed ghosts of love
That life, for lack of something
    Simple as a clothespin,
        Let fall, one by one.

THE ROCK

Year after year he returned to the same
Spot, hoping for a change. But found
No change, except that sometimes
The water was darker, sometimes
The beach was littered, sometimes not.

Month after month he thought as he
Imagined the journey back,
This time all will be different,
This time the rock will stand free,
Pushed back the shrouding sea.

But always, except that sometimes
The water tossed darker, sometimes
As light as cloud, the sea
Would reach the place on the rock
His head had dashed with blood.

And this distressed him. For
If the sea was changeless,
Except for the color, except for
The look of the beach, he was not.
As he saw when bent across

The rock, his face a scum upon
The moving water. Yet year
After year he came back to look again,
Until the bloodstain on the rock
Was like a sleeping eye, washed

By the hissing foam, until they had
To hold him as he scraped across
The sand. Dropping their pails
Below the rock like explorers
Come to the one and only place.

And made a castle there beside
The rock. Year after year
The grandchildren returned, and saw
The water lapping on the rock,
And thought of him, and thought of death.

Part III

From *The Pit*
and Other Poems (1969)

OEUVRE

Will it ever be finished, this house
  Of paper
I began to raise when I was seventeen?

Others scramble from foundations far less firm.
  Seasons of
Pondering, name by name, the past's magnificent,

A squandering. Surely I might have lived.
  Spitefully
Watching as rivals stole the girls, got the jobs,

Won the laurels, the misery seeped in,
  Tinting the
Windows, darkening the fairest day.

But how should I have known, a house to please
  Need not be
Outlandish? And that searching everywhere

The fresh, the rare, prowling the gaudier
  Capitals,
Something of each would rub off, deface.

Well, we build where and as we can. There are
  Days when I
Am troubled by an image of the house,

Laden, rootless, like a tinseled tree,
  Suddenly
Torn to a thousand scribbled leaves and borne off

By the wind, then to be gathered and patched
  Whole again,
Or of the thing going up in smoke

And I, the paper dreamer, wide awake.

TO A JAPANESE POET

You stood frozen there,
One hand gripping my arm,
In the other your lunchbasket,
And when I turned
To look into your face,
It was like witnessing a birth.

When the poem came,
Your fingers loosened and you
Spoke the dozen words as if
Directing one who'd
Lost his way upon
A mountain path, the night descending.

Finally we went to join
The others, but you were not the same.
All that brilliant autumn day
You avoided me
As if I'd surprised you
In some intimacy, as if my being

Near had suddenly
Cut us off. Later, when I mentioned
A hurt no memory of scarlet leaves
Could ease, you laughed
And said, "Why should you
Have felt badly? We had an enjoyable outing."

ZEN: THE ROCKS OF SESSHU

(Joei Temple Garden, Yamaguchi)

I

What do they think of
   Where they lean
Like ponderous heads, the rocks?—

In prankish spring, ducks
   Joggling here
And there, brushing tails,

Like silly thoughts shared,
   Passed from head
To head? When, gong quavering

About a ripened sky, we
   Up and go,
Do they waken from a dream of flesh?

II

In the Three Whites of
   Hokusai—
Fuji, the snow, the crane—

What startles is the black: in
   The outline
Of the mountain, the branch-tips

Piercing the snow, the quills of
   The crane's wing:
Meaning impermanence.

Here, in stainless air, the
   Artist's name
Blazes like a crow.

44

III

Distance between the rocks,
  Half the day
In shadow, is the distance

Between man who thinks
  And the man
Who thinks he thinks: wait.

Like a brain, the garden,
  Thinking when
It is thought. Otherwise

A stony jumble, merely that,
  Laid down there
To stud our emptiness.

IV

Who calls her butterfly
  Would elsewhere
Pardon the snake its fangs:

In the stony garden
  Where she flits
Are sides so sharp, merely

To look gives pain. Only
  The tourist,
Kodak aimed and ready for

The blast, ship pointing for the
  Getaway,
Dare raise that parasol.

V

To rid the grass of weed, to get
   The whole root,
Thick, tangled, takes a strong mind

And desire—to make clean, make pure.
   The weed, tough
As the rock it leaps against,

Unless plucked to the last
   Live fiber
Will plunge up through dark again.

The weed also has the desire
   To make clean,
Make pure, there against the rock.

VI

It is joy that lifts those pigeons to
   Stitch the clouds
With circling, light flashing from underwings.

Scorning our crumbs, tossed carefully
   To corners
Of the garden, beyond the rocks,

They rose as if summoned from
   The futile
Groveling our love subjects them to.

Clear the mind! Empty it of all that
   Fixes you,
Makes every act a pecking at the crumb.

VII

Firmness is all: that mountain beyond the
     Garden path,
Watch how against its tawny slope

The candled boughs expire. Follow
     The slope where
Spearheads shake against the clouds

And dizzy the pigeons circling on the wind.
     Then observe
Where no bigger than a cragstone

The climber pulls himself aloft,
     As by the
Very guts: firmness is all.

VIII

Pierced through by birdsong, stone by stone
     The garden
Gathered light. Darkness, hauled by ropes

Of sun, entered roof and bough. Raised from
     The temple
Floor where, stiff since cockcrow,

Blown round like Buddha on the lotus,
     He began
To write. How against that shimmering,

On paper frail as dawn, make poems?
     Firm again,
He waited for the rocks to split.

THE QUAKE

Alone in that paper house
We laughed when the bed
Heaved twice then threw
Us to the floor. When all

Was calm again, you said
It took an earthquake
To untwine us. Then I
Stopped your shaking

With my mouth. Together
In this place of brick,
Held firm as fruits
Upon a sculptured bough,

Our loving is more safe.
Then why should dream
Return us to that fragile
Shelf of land? And why,

Our bodies twined upon
This couch of stone,
Should we be listening,
Like dead sinners, for the quake?

H. S. WITH NOH MASK

Unpacking again, tired, fearing
        Another drought,
You plunge an arm into the trunk

And, holding the mask against your
        Face, stand before
The mirror searching the self

I made you leave behind: dark hair
        Flowing with its
Three loose strands, eyes burning back

To where you always are, cheeks
        Like sides of tusks
And there, through parted lips

The squares of blackened teeth which
        Alone are strange.
How naturally you pose in time

Back here in Chicago
        Where tomorrow,
Noh mask hung upon the wall,

You must try to make a life.

RETURN TO DEKALB

Expecting no miracle, we found none:
One retarred blacktop, another supermart,
        The sum of change—

Apart from the waiting neighbors, in which
Plentiful loss of hair and swollen girth,
        Those additions

To a catalogue of woes, came as small
Surprise. We were the lucky travelers
        Come back to plan

A further flight, happy to learn that none
Remembered an earthquake in Persia or
    Rioting in Greece.

Suddenly sick of so much reality,
We climbed the long-worn staircase to the
    Bedroom, and found

What each had thought was shaken off—Time
Rose stinking from the mattress, perched, a
    Raven, on the sill.

THE ANNIVERSARY

The sun rising,
  The sun setting,
Takes no more beauty
  On than yours
Whom the years have
  Carried like a vessel
Across the grinding seas.

I ride you like
  A Sinbad, seeking
What I have but
  Cannot find until
The Roc lies plucked
  And bleeding on
The shore all sailors curse.

O love, this ten years'
  Voyage in your arms
Has taught me nothing
  That I did not know
When, sighting you, I swam
  To board the one fair ship
Among the blistered prows.

VOYAGER

And how he pities the man with an arm
About the girl who, like a tug, guides
Him through the high sea of aloneness,
Certain to toss him on the nearest shore,

Should another beckon. Forever solitary,
How he feels for those that go, two by two,
In the illusion of togetherness.
Watching outside the Greyhound Station

For the carriage that will take him anywhere,
He is part of all: in every city
Painted mouths are pouting to be bruised,
A thousand sheets, stretching like a snowfield,

Await the restless imprint of his limbs.
The voyager can cherish the heart fulfilled
For its illusion of fulfillment
As he moves in the dream of arrival.

LOVER

Always the exile
Learning a strange landscape,
    Unsure

Of self, certain only
Of the moon, despite her
    New face

And the memory,
Vaguely troubling as
    Her light,

Of promises in
A country true
    As this.

ÉTUDE

I was cycling by the river, back and forth,
    Umbrella up against the
        Rain and blossoms.

It was very quiet, I thought of Woolworth
    Globes you shake up snowstorms in.
        Washed light slanted

Through the cherry trees, and in a flimsy house
    Some youngster practiced Chopin.
        I was moving

With the current, wheels squishing as the music
    Rose into the trees, then stopped,
        And from the house

Came someone wearing too much powder, raincape
    Orchid in the light. Middle-aged,
        The sort you pass

In hundreds everyday and scarcely notice,
    The Chopin she had sent
        Up to those boughs,

Petals spinning free, gave her grace no waters
    Would reflect, but I might
        Long remember.

THAT WOMAN THERE

Will she ever go away, that woman there?
Every night she stands with arms upraised,
High throat twisting in the streetlamp's noose.

One by one they come, the wild beseechers—
Merchants, students, thieves, he who squats before,
Shaking a bouquet of dollars at her knees.

O she is cruel to keep them, eyes plucking
At these half-drawn blinds. What does she hope
To offer, fingers spread, sharp heels grinding?

Must she be told that He has left for good?

SONG FOR ONE

After the wedding,
The flung rice and boots,
    The guests like fountains
Gushing on the lawn
        (Her arms around him
        Like a noose)
It was good to get out of town,
        Lay her down
    In the dark of a room
He would never see again.

    After the honeymoon,
Niagara and the Empire State,
    The coins and tokens
Pelting from his purse

(Her body like a doe
Lashed to a hood)
It was sad to get back to town,
Lay her down
In the dark of a room
He had hated from the start.

THE LOCUSTS

Whirring from the desert, so dense
We thought the sand
Was heaving to engulf us,

The locusts raised a wind. Sunlight
Scarcely filtered
Through, then, sudden decimator,

The car made paste-and-membrane
Of their swarming,
Trophied where a hundred spanning

Wings and wrenched sky-hopping legs
Had clung. We moved
Through famished miles, blind, remembered

Plagues as thick and foul about us.
Reaching town, I
Hosed the car down for a day,

Then sold it. Today whenever
I think of her,
Locusts, locusts, break around me.

OBJET D'ART

The copper bowl I keep
        Tobacco
In is thick with nightingales

And roses, up to the
        Minaret
Its lid, incised so-so.

I no longer smoke in
        Company,
It seems indecent:

Reminded by those birds
        And flowers
Of a botched renown,

A Persian I once
        Had for tea
Turned from it and wept.

SNOWS

I

All night thick flakes have fallen,
The street below lies smothered
        With the past.
One remembers other snows
        (Images
In snapshots framed by the chill
Edge), ablaze before the thaw.

II

Disburdenment is what mind seeks
Above all other riches,
      Disburdenment
Of little griefs gathered like drifts
Into each corner. I think of
      This as, shovel
Arcing wide, breath peopling the air,
I hurl slosh like diamonds at
      A snout of sun.

TREES

I

For five years now
I've caught you
At your tricks,

Marveling as you've
Stirred after the brown
Death, the white.

Envious, I watch
You where the
Words don't come—

Remembering
A quick flame,
The settling of ash.

II

All day the powersaws whir,
Sick trees come down, festering
      The walk with limbs.

The old street stretches to cornfields
Like an amputee. Above the
    Rip-tooth clamor

Of a long-awaited spring,
Birds wheel like exiles in
    A time of war.

IMAGE

The house
Huge ugly plant
Peeling rotting
Around us
Making dark dark
Draining
Cutting off
It will see
Our end
Its floorboards
Sinking
To our dead weight

MEMO TO THE BUILDER

... and then
After the roof goes up
Remember to lay the eave trough
Wide and deep. A run
For squirrels and a river
For my birds. You know, I'd rather

You made the trough
So, than have the rooftop

Tarred and shingled. Keep
It in mind, the trough.
Also I'm not so sure of glass
In every window. But let that pass.

Still—and there are
Reasons enough, believe me—
It would please no end to be
In and out together.
And how it would thrill me should a bird,
Learning our secret, make a whir-

ring thoroughfare
Of a room or two.
Forget the weather. To
Have the wild, the rare
Not only happen, mind, but
Be the normal is exactly what

I'm after. Now
You know. Perhaps you
Think I've made your job too
Light? Good. Throw
Caution to the beams. Build me a home
The living day can enter, not a tomb.

CROW

He is made giddy by the sun,
And is stupid enough to race
Its rise and fall, so that at dawn

One spots him lumbering across the
Winter sky, then perched like a heart
Within the skeletal tree.

Wherever he goes he carries
His stomach like a weapon,
And the small bird hungering flies

In his wake, hoping for a crumb
As the foul beak chews and caws
Together and the black wings climb.

Devourer of acres, he drops
On the puny scarecrow and plants
Tomorrow's morsel between the flaps

Of its straw-stuck coat. Nothing
Frightens him, the hawk will whirl
From what he swoops for, this king

Of field and fat metropolis.
And already taken over
From the eagle, he must replace

That ancient master of the sky
On escutcheon and dollar.
In this usurpation he

Most resembles us: image of
Our gutty need and power, he
Merits all our rubbish and our love.

CORMORANT

Men speak lightly of frustration,
As if they'd invented it.

As if like the cormorant
Of Gifu, thick leg roped, a ring

Cutting into the neck, they dived
All night to the fish-swelled water

And flapped up with the catch lodged
In the throat, only to have

The fisher yank it out and toss
It gasping on a breathless heap.

Then to dive again, hunger
Churning in the craw, air just

Slipping by the throat-ring
To spray against the lungs.

And once more to be jerked back in
And have the fisher grab the spoil.

Men speak lightly of frustration,
And dim in the lantern light

The cormorant makes out the flash
Of fins and, just beyond,

The streamered boats of tourists
Rocking under *saké* fumes.

JACKAL

That he springs from a hole
And sniffs along the pit
For garbage delectable

Is no distinction: this any
Dog can do. And does. That
He flies at man-smell, canny

At hiding in places made
For roaches and the smallest
Mice, is not so very odd.

The sharp dividing line,
What makes us think of him
As neither out nor in,

Neither wild nor tractable
Is, first of all, his bark
Which is the laugh of a fool

Pulled out at midnight from
A reeking bed, and then
The outlaw look of him

As caught in the flashlight's shine,
Thin legs straddling something foul,
He yelps and bolts the town.

THE SQUIRREL

Gray fur to brown earth,
    The grasses clinging,
Eyes still bright, piercing

Through those topmost boughs
    Where, choked with nuts,
It clambered to the sun.

The rat has come to gnaw,
    The dog to sniff,
And I to meet my death:

Gray flesh to brown earth,
    The grasses clinging,
Eyes still bright, piercing

Through those tangled roots
    Where, crazed with fear,
I leapt from shade to shade.

THE LIBERATOR

Approaching the laboratory gate
He heard familiar squeals and, again,
Myriad rat's feet along maze-planks,
Then crows, yelps, mews: he was
Climbing the gangway of the Ark,
The Deluge boiling round his knees.

Entering, he glanced back where
The smashed glass door reflected head
And wobbly shins: the rest of him he
Must have left out in the drunken
Dark. Plucked on by cries of those he'd
Come to save, he passed frothed rows

Of test tubes, pickled embryos.
A swipe of the arm, and down they crashed,
Slicking the concrete floor. Still
The living urged him on: Out! Out!
It was a cry he'd learned to
Understand. When he reached the

Guinea pigs, unsnapped the toolbox
Lid and sheared the cage-wire, they licked,
All gratitude, the palm that
Offered crumbs. The rats, when sprung,
Scurried dizzily across the
Table strewn with cheese he'd cached

For weeks. And now, no longer
Running wild, the cocks, mongrels, cats
Fed beak by jowl together.
High above them on a stool, he
Smiled the smile of God, first
Work done, betrayals yet to come.

THE FINAL SLOPE

Climbing the final slope
He thought of them below
Ledged with the rancid goats.
    Two hundred feet to go,
Their envy snapping on the rope,

He spat into the sun.
Then the mountain threw him:
Like a butcher's beast he hung,
    Lashed to a crazy limb,
By pride and the wind undone.

By pride and the wind undone,
Legs swinging far beneath,
He felt the goats and their kids
    Nibbling at his feet,
And the sun's beak in his bone.

LIFEGUARD

All day they crush around his pedestal,
   Whiteness smoking on the bone,
      Lotioned fat

Of sacrifice. The sandgirls ogling up
   Like carp would shimmer gladly
      In his net.

You who lounge about them in this sweat,
   Enjoy while there is time what
      Soon must leap

To snare and snaring stay, to whelp across
   His strand a siege of castle
      Captains. Act

Before those waves, tall henchmen of his eyes,
   Cut in and drag the darlings
      To his arms.

AND THEY CALL THIS LIVING!

The sea that morning was as unruffled
As a tub of dirty water,
But we couldn't find the plug.
All right, we said, let it sit,
Let the gull keep dropping to the scum.

Then our son came running running
With one hand held up high. All right,
We said, let him dream a stained eyetooth
Right out of the Leviathan's jaw.
He's glad, and what have we got to lose?

And all right, we said, let the sun
Burn down at will. We'll furl
The striped umbrella and let it do
Its worst. For once, we said, accept
The ruddy show just as it's always been:

The sea as so much liquid having
Nowhere else to go, an eyetooth
Some old peddler fished from a nosebag
As a relic to be bragged at school
And the sun the navel of us all.

Then just as sure as we were
Sprawling there, a wind sprang up
To knock the sea for loops
And spin the fishers in their smacks,
And the eyetooth started shrinking.

All right, we said, grabbing the kid
And unfurling the striped umbrella.
All right, all right as the sunburn started
Itching and we buried the eyetooth
In the sand—next time we'll know better.

SON

I no longer please him; he's found heroes
Whose exploits, of whatever style or magnitude,
Outstrip my own. Swinging a bat, running,
Shooting, you'd expect to be surpassed.

But it's also in the poems he reads,
Thoughts he cannot quite decipher.
Sometimes I hate what's dragged him
From my knees to lour before me,

Lofty with idols left and right,
Denying the castoff what shouldn't
Be denied a dog. Well, we grow, move off,
Despising all that's kept us from

Those misted vales and outlands
Roamed by dragons and redolent of maidens
Until, all heroes fallen,
We steal back home to clasp the only

Certain thing: which is no longer there.

I. M. JEAN COCTEAU

Who would bury
What did not
   Exist?

A puff of opium
Held over
   Seventy

Years between
The fat cheeks of
   Paris,

Your expiration
Dizzies and
   Bereaves.

PARIS

With fifty thousand daubers
To paint your face, you will never
Grow old, they say, with as many lovelies
Legging up your squares, you will
Always gratify, they say, O with your river
      And your bridges and your quays,
The mind need never wander to the north,
The east, the west, nor settle in the azured south,
      They say.

Yet ask any two Frenchmen
Spawned on the cobbles of whatever
Dreary *arrondissement,* ask them at the hour
The terraces are emptied of their tables,
The chairs piled high, the sidewalks scoured,
      And looking to the north, the east,
The west, finally to the brilliant
South, they'll say *Merde!* and *Merde!* again. That's what
      They say.

Ah, to one spawned on the asphalt
Of whatever American city, it is sweetest comfort
To know that, stripped of the décor, your gargoyles
      Pulled down (O hear the tourists sobbing in the choir!),
Bereft of the fifty thousand palettes and the
      Innumerable brushes that hide your face,
You are no more ugly than that garish
Daughter who, after plying fabulously the Champs Elysées,
      They say,

Ended up, five years later
Under a gaslight in Les Halles. *Zut alors!*
I'd rather be a banker in Duluth, with a Swede
Wife and two cars in the garage, than a
Boulevardier with ten *sous* in the pocket, a head gone
      Soft with dreaming north, east, west and south,
And a kept bitch that cheers the porter in a
Greasy bed. *Mon Dieu! c'est triste la vie, n'est-ce pas?*
      They say.

AT VIRGIL'S TOMB

The bus stops just outside the gate
        Where all day long
The kids retrieve their soccer ball.

I watch and wait (in Ravenna
        Your Florentine
Lay starred on every tourist's map,

And gendarmes' pikes, like gladioli,
        Blazed around him).
Now as the tour-bus honks below

I imagine another Beatrice
        Entreating you,
In glory's dream, to guide her lover

Through that flaming labyrinth.
        At last you speak:
"Tell him to live remembering you,

Say that long ago man's boot ground through
        Inferno's crust,
The world he made, and will not know."

LINES ON AN 18TH C. TAPESTRY

It is a very pretty scene:
        As in a picture by Watteau,
The lovers seem about
        To strip themselves of all
Stiff finery and teach the faun

That stamps within the wood
    What violence a parcel
Of gallants bestirred, can wreak
    Upon a summer's greensward frail
With damsels of the blood.

On a damask stained with wine
    The ribboned marmosets devour
Such nibbled fruits and broken cakes
    That, envious in the wing-bright air,
The starlings cluster to complain.

His face uplifted to the sky,
    A lackey strums a mandolin,
But how should they attend harsh strings
    Who hear the song of flesh and bone
Stealing through their finery?

THE DREAM

He entered a zoo of reptiles
    Uncaged but chained,
Each with familiar face,
    Voice, claim on him.
The sunlight flashed off
    Scaly backs, earth
Clung to slimed jaws, the path wove
    Through and round them
From entrance to far wall—
    Dark, uneven.
But what most astonished as
    He passed the beasts
Was the cunning in the chains:
    Try as they might,
Muscles heaping, to claw beyond
    His shadow, which

Torn to strips of earth
　　Was flung aside,
They could not. However single and
　　Intense their claim,
However paws struck out, he passed
　　Them unafraid:
Those chains rang solidly where they'd been
　　Pegged in concrete.
His peace was like that of
　　The tamer who,
After years of waltzing
　　With the same cats,
Could lie for hours, head
　　Between their fangs.
When he slipped the last of them,
　　He came upon
A harem lined up in scale
　　Of nakedness,
Faces like those one sees in
　　Northern cities
Sharp at noon when shops and offices
　　Debouch onto
The churning streets for sandwiches and
　　Coffee. The first
Seemed very proper, and in one
　　Or another
He recognized a classmate
　　For whom he'd itched,
Head in arms, eyes swung back
　　And climbing thighs
And into panties like sacks
　　Of tropic fruit.
Yet unlike the reptiles these made no
　　Move toward him.
They tried to win him
　　With demureness,
Never mind as he strode on the ripped
　　Skirts, blouses slashed

To midriffs. He knew them all,
    Just as they were,
With his lost fantastic eyes that were
    Always peering
Through and far beyond. And now it
    Was only fair
To pick one out and, he supposed,
    Save her from him
Whose chains would be the first to
    Give. Like a vain
Commander he went slowly by
    The lot, pinching
Here, patting there, then stood before
    The last of all,
Who posed, small hands raising
    Breasts, his mother's.
He rushed off, cheated, muttering,
    The smell so sharp
He must escape at once,
    And damn the lot.
At the wall the roaring
    Swelled where the beasts
Were strained and pawing at
    His back, the clang
Of chains like knells in
    A year of plague.
But the gate had disappeared.
    He groped along
The wall, which was horny to
    The touch and patched
With scales that formed
    Footholds, handgrips.
He leapt and slowly mounted,
    Fingers oozing,
Until at last he stared down at the
    Sea. The roaring
Ceased. He dived and woke to blackness.

VOGUE

Your women are judged beautiful:
Their underarms are hairless, legs
    And netherzones.

Clamped to their breasts are tiny
Rubber shields and, circling low,
    Those sheering walls

No arrow yet has pierced, only
Gold pulls down. Your women
    Go unrivaled:

Impenetrable as fortresses
They line those cold medieval streets
    No charger dares.

How you must weep to see them giving
Suck, your daughters, to dolls
    Of flesh and blood.

CHRIST OF PERSHING SQUARE

"I can prove it!" the madman cried
And clutched my wrist. "Feel where the nails
Went in! By God, I bear them still!"

Half amused, I shrugged and let him
Press the hand against his suture:
"All right," I said, "they cut you up."

Suddenly those fingers grasped
A hammer, it was I had hoisted
The cross his flung arms formed there.

"Yet," I whispered, "there remains
The final proof—forgiveness."
He spat into my face and fled.

This happened in Los Angeles
Six months ago. I see him still,
White blood streaming, risen from

Cancerous sheets to walk a Kingdom.

LAMENT FOR WELDON KEES

Could we have known that torrid night
A book of yours would sell
For eighteen dollars, we might

Have gotten a little drunker.
Weldon, where the blazes are you?
I can't help thinking of your

Wife, the lovely way she
Had of listening, holding her
Pride in you like a virginity.

We talked of poems, your "Robinson,"
And then you shuffled back
To slap some more paint down,

The canvas flat upon the table,
Under a light so fierce I thought
The paint would run. You didn't call

It that, but painting was your hackwork,
And surely the hope of poet's ease
Held you there from dark to dark,

The gin beside you on a stool.
I was green as grass, and you
My first live poet. What a bloody fool

You must have thought me! But it
Wasn't your praise I wanted then,
And thank Christ you knew that.

Just to be with you, and talk,
And drink your gin was what I'd
Come for. I left your room to walk

The city ragged, knowing at last
That poets were quite human.
Later, when I heard that you were lost,

Your car found parked too near the bridge,
I wondered which of us had left it there.
By then I too was hanging from the edge.

THE CANNERY

In summer this town is full of rebels
Come up from Tennessee to shell the peas.

And wetbacks roam the supermarts, making
A Tijuana of the drab main street.

The Swedes and Poles who work at Wurlitzer,
And can't stand music, are all dug in:

Doors are bolted, their pretty children warned,
Where they wait for the autumnal peace.

At night the cannery's like a train,
A runaway, cans flung up like clinkers.

Sometimes on an evening hot as Southland
When even fear won't keep the windows down,

One hears the drawl of Tennessee, the quick
Laugh of Mexico in the empty streets.

TO AN ASTRONAUT

Drink up! The night's a cave
Whose mouth, the moon,
Wastes to a hair's-breadth
Then is lost in clouds.

And who are you to climb
Such steeps of sky, where
Huge on hills of frozen
Light, the gods are ravening

And jealous angels, wakened
By your knocking, gather
Hailstones and the chunkiest
Pips of heaven to pelt

You as you rise? Already
Certain saints pray for you
In futurity, confused
By an image pierced

With the silver metals
Of its fall to martyrdom.
And those departed ones
Who shaped you lovingly

For this one terrible role
(And thereby entered Paradise)
Kneel in readiness
With wreaths and mute hosannas

At the icy tombstone
Each has wept for you.
Drink up! I say.
The gods roar, ravening.

SPEECH TO THE SHAPERS

They are wrong who think the end will be
Violent, rank alarmists who have
Visions of bombs bursting east and west
Together, leaving their hillocks of

Dead. Or who sniff already in the
Wind the poisons that will circle and
Devour. They have not lived enough who
See great armies joined along a strand

By nothing more than the bayonets
They'd stabbed into each other's innards,
With, to complete the savage picture,
Vultures and, moored with flesh, the buzzards.

And what must one really think of those
Who leap from Bibles reciting Doom,
When not only every Doom so far
Recited has failed, like rain, to come

But even the callowest Sunday
Schooler grins? The end will steal upon
Us as an average day, sometime between
Breakfast and lunch, while Father is down

At the office, Junior playing ball
And Mother is choosing lambchops at
The butcher's. Unannounced, it will drop
From a cloudless sky, or like a cut

In the power take us by surprise,
With all the lights snuffed out together.
But far more than the lights will go out,
And whatever's wrong will not appear

To be wrong, and it will have begun not
The day before, or now, or even
A thousand years ago. There's the rub.
We'll never know what hit us where, or when.

STEVE CRAWLEY

Why whenever they mention Hawaii
Do I think of you, and not the hula
Girls or orchids shrill against the blue?
Why when they send postcards of tourists tense
Around a burning pig, leis like collars
On a brace of hounds, do I see you flung
Across the earthfloor of that tent again,
Brains like macaroni puddled at the ear?

Steve Crawley, we found her letter crushed
Between the oilcan and the rosary
On your cot, and thought we understood,
But what puzzles still is this: what were you
Doing in that cathouse line, all brass
And itch, the night before the letter came?

THE PIT

Twenty years. I still remember
The sun-blown stench, and the pit
At least two hundred yards from
The cove we'd anchored guns in.
They were blasting at the mountains,
The beach was nearly ours.

The smell kept leaking back.
I thought of garbage cans
Behind chopsuey restaurants
Of home, strangely appealing on
A summer's night, meaning another
Kind of life. Which made the difference.

When the three of us, youngest in
The crew, were handed poles and told
To get the deadmen underground
Or join them, we saw it a sullen
Sort of lark. And lashed to trees,
The snipers had us dancing.

Ducks for those vultures in the boughs,
Poles poking through the powder-
Bitten grass, we zigzagged
Toward the pit as into
The arse of death, the wittiest
Of us said but did not laugh.

At last we reached it, half full
Of sand and crawling. We clamped
Nose, mouth, wrenched netted helmets
To the chin, yet poles probed forward
Surgically, touching for spots
The maggots had not jelled.

Somehow we got the deadmen under,
Along with empty lobster tins,
Bottles, gear and ammo. Somehow
We plugged the pit and slipped back
To the guns. Then for days
We had to helmet bathe downwind.

I stuck my pole, clean end high,
Behind the foxhole, a kind of
Towelpeg and a something more.
I'd stare it out through jungle haze,
And wonder. Ask anyone who
Saw it: nobody won that war.

Part IV

From *Afterimages: Zen Poems of Shinkichi Takahashi* (1970)

A WOOD IN SOUND

The pinetree sways in the smoke,
Which streams up and up.
There's a wood in sound.

My legs lose themselves
Where the river mirrors daffodils
Like faces in a dream.

A cold wind and the white memory
Of a sasanqua.
Warm rain comes and goes.

I'll wait calmly on the bank
Till the water clears
And willows start to bud.

Time is singed on the debris
Of air raids.
Somehow, here and now, I am another.

ACHING OF LIFE

There must be something better,
But I'm satisfied just as I am.

Monkeys sport deep in the forest,
Fish shoot up the mountain stream.

If there's change, there's also repose—
Which soon must suffer change.

Along the solar orbit of the night,
I feel life's constant aching:

Smack in the middle of the day,
I found moonlight between a woman's legs.

SNOW WIND

There's nothing more to see:
Snow in the nandin's leaves
And, under it, the red-eyed
Rabbit lies frozen.

I'll place everything on
Your eyeballs, the universe.
There's nothing more to see:
Nandin berries are red, snow white.

The rabbit hopped twice in the cool
Breeze and everyone disappeared,
Leaving the barest scent.
The horizon curves endlessly

And now there's no more light
Around the rabbit's body.
Suddenly your face
Is large as the universe.

CANNA

A red canna blooms,
While between us flickers
A death's head, dancing there
Like a pigmy or tiny ball.

We try to catch it—
Now it brushes my hands,
Now dallies with her feet.

She often talks of suicide.
Scared, I avoid her cold face.

Again today she spoke
Of certain premonitions.
How can I possibly
Save this woman's life?

Living as if dead, I shall
Give up my own. She must live.

TIME

Time like a lake breeze
Touched his face,
All thought left his mind.

One morning the sun, menacing,
Rose from behind a mountain,
Singeing—like hope—the trees.

Fully awakened, he lit his pipe
And assumed the sun-inhaling pose:
Time poured down—like rain, like fruit.

He glanced back and saw a ship
Moving towards the past. In one hand
He gripped the sail of eternity,

And stuffed the universe into his eyes.

84

THE PINK SUN

White petals on the black earth,
Their scent filling her nostrils.

Breathe out and all things swell—
Breathe in, they shrink.

Let's suppose she suddenly has four legs—
That's far from fantastic.

I'll weld ox hoofs onto her feet—
Sparks of the camellia's sharp red.

Wagging her pretty little tail,
She's absorbed in kitchenwork.

Look, she who just last night
Was a crone is girl again,

An alpine rose blooming on her arm.
High on a Himalayan ridge

The great King of Bhutan
Snores in the pinkest sun.

THISTLES

Thistles bloomed in the vast moonlit
Cup of the Mexican sands.

Thistles bloomed on the round hillock
Of a woman's heart.

The stained sea was choked with thistles,
Sky stowed away in thistle stalks.

Thistles, resembling a male corpse, bloomed
Like murex from a woman's side.

At the thorny root of a yellow cactus plant
A plucked pigeon crouched,

And off in the distance a dog whimpered,
As if swallowing hot air.

RAT ON MOUNT ISHIZUCHI

Snow glitters on the divine rocks
At the foot of Mount Ishizuchi.
Casting its shadow on the mountain top,
A rat flies off.

At the back of the sun,
Where rats pound rice into cakes,
There's a cavity like a mortar pit.

A flyer faster than an airplane,
That's the sparrow.
Mount Ishizuchi, too, flies at a devilish speed,
Ten billion miles a second,
From everlasting to everlasting.

Yet, because there's no time,
And always the same dusk,
It doesn't fly at all:
The peak of Mount Ishizuchi
Has straightened the spine
Of the Island of Futana.

Because there's no space
The airplane doesn't move an inch:
The sun, the plane boarded by the rat,
Are afloat in the sparrow's dream.

BURNING ONESELF TO DEATH

That was the best moment of the monk's life.
Firm on a pile of firewood
With nothing more to say, hear, see,
Smoke wrapped him, his folded hands blazed.

There was nothing more to do, the end
Of everything. He remembered, as a cool breeze
Streamed through him, that one is always
In the same place, and that there is no time.

Suddenly a whirling mushroom cloud rose
Before his singed eyes, and he was a mass
Of flame. Globes, one after another, rolled out,
The delighted sparrows flew round like fire balls.

BACK YARD

The sky clears after rain,
Yellow roses glistening in the light.
Crossing two thresholds, the cat moves off.

Your back is overgrown with nandin leaves.
How awkward your gait!
Like a chicken on damp leaves.
Your necktie, made from skin
Of a tropical fighting fish,
Is hardly subdued. Your yolk-colored
Coat will soon be dyed
With blood again, like a cock's crest.

Let your glances pierce
Like a hedgehog's spines,
I reject them. I can't imagine
What would happen if our glances met.

One day I'll pulverize you.
Now you're scratching
In the bamboo roots, famished.
Watch it—I'll toss you down a hole.

With your cockspurs you kick off
Mars, earth, mankind,
All manner of things, then
Pick over them with your teeth.

Atomic horses bulge through
The pores of a peach-like girl.
The persimmon's leaves are gone again.

THE PIPE

While I slept it was all over,
Everything. My eyes, squashed white,
Flowed off toward dawn.

There was a noise,
Which, like all else, spread and disappeared:
There's nothing worth seeing, listening for.

When I woke, everything seemed cut off.
I was a pipe, still smoking,
Which daylight would knock empty once again.

CROW

The crow, spreading wide wings,
Flapped lazily off.
Soon her young will be doing the same,
Firm wings rustling.

It's hard to tell the male
Crow from the female,
But their love, their mating
Must be fresh as their flight.

Asleep in a night train,
I felt my hat fly off.
The crow was lost in mist,
The engine ploughed into the sea.

WHITE FLOWER

One flower, my family and I,
And I but a petal.
I grasp a hoe in one hand,
Wife and child by the other.

It wasn't I who drove that stake
Into the earth, then pulled it out.
I'm innocent—rather we are,
Like that white cloud above.

I stretch out my right hand: nothing.
I raise my left: nobody.
A white flower opens,
And now I stand apart

While, above, a bomber soars.
My family and I are buried alive.
I'm a handful of earth.
Untraceable.

MUMMY

Resuscitated
By the kiss of a bat
On its papyrus mouth
And the Nile's spring thrust,
The mummy arose amidst
The jolting pillars
And strode from the cave,
Followed by a throng of bats.

Tripping on a pyramid step,
The mummy was landed upon
By a bat, a sarcophagus lid,
Who, by patting its head with her wing,
Unwound the mummy's cloth,
Dipped it in the Nile,
Then wrapped it round herself
From claw-tips to shoulders.
She lay down—a mummy.

Tail up, the sphinx came
To sniff her all over,
But the bat was fast asleep.
How many centuries have slipped by?
The dam's dried up,
This once submerged temple
Stands again,
Its stone birds
Have once more taken flight.

RED WAVES

A cat, a black-white tabby out of nowhere,
Licks its back at the water's edge:
Perhaps—with that bit of metal dangling
From her middle—a space cat,
Readying to fly off again.

But how to ask her? I opened my hand, wide,
Just in front of her face, at which
She flipped over, legs up and pointing
Toward the sea in the pose of a "beckoning cat."

The sea obliged: she was carried off
Bobbing on the waves. Was she drowned?
I asked myself over and over,
Alone for hours on the moonlit beach.

Suddenly a red parasol came rolling
Toward me—the cat's? It danced along
The windless shore, with me chasing full tilt.
I didn't have a chance. Come daybreak
I spotted the parasol rising above a rock:
The sun, blinding! Red waves reached my ankles.

DESTRUCTION

The universe is forever falling apart—
No need to push the button,
It collapses at a finger's touch:
Why, it barely hangs on the tail of a sparrow's eye.

The universe is so much eye secretion,
Hordes leap from the tips
Of your nostril hairs. Lift your right hand:
It's in your palm. There's room enough

On the sparrow's eyelash for the whole.

A paltry thing, the universe:
Here is all strength, here the greatest strength.
You and the sparrow are one
And, should he wish, he can crush you.
The universe trembles before him.

DISCLOSURE

The sparrow sleeps, thinking of nothing.
Meanwhile the universe has shrunk to half.
He's attached by a navel string, swimming
In a sea of fluid, amniotic, slightly bitter.

The center is "severance"—no sound at all—
Until the navel string is snapped. All of which
Was told by her as she sat astride Pegasus,
The poet on a circuit of the universe.

The sparrow came at her, bill like a sword,
And suddenly from her buttocks—the sun!
The sparrow carried the stained sheets
To the moon. On drawing the clouds apart,

He discovered the cold corpse of Mars.
Not once had he disclosed the secrets of his life.

WHAT IS MOVING

When I turned to look back
Over the waters
The sky was birdless.

Men *were, are* born.
Do I still live? I ask myself,
Munching a sweet potato.

Don't smell of death,
Don't cast its shadow.
Any woman when I glance her way,
Looks down,
Unable to stand it.
Men, as if dead,
Turn up the whites of their eyes.

Get rid of those trashy ideas—
The same thing
Runs through both of us.
My thought moves the world:
I move, it moves.
I crook my arm, the world's crooked.

THE PEACH

A little girl under a peach tree,
Whose blossoms fall into the entrails
Of the earth.

There you stand, but a mountain may be there
Instead; it is not unlikely that the earth
May be yourself.

You step against a plate of iron and half
Your face is turned to iron. I will smash
Flesh and bone

And suck the cracked peach. She went up the mountain
To hide her breasts in the snowy ravine.
Women's legs

Are more or less alike. The leaves of the peach tree
Stretch across the sea to the end of
The continent.

The sea was at the little girl's beck and call.
I will cross the sea like a hairy
Caterpillar

And catch the odor of your body.

QUAILS

It is the grass that moves, not the quails.
Weary of embraces, she thought of
Committing her body to the flame.

When I shut my eyes, I hear far and wide
The air of the Ice Age stirring.
When I open them, a rocket passes over a meteor.

A quail's egg is complete in itself,
Leaving not room enough for a dagger's point.
All the phenomena in the universe: myself.

Quails are supported by the universe
(I wonder if that means subsisting by God).
A quail has seized God by the neck

With its black bill, because there is no
God greater than a quail.
(Peter, Christ, Judas: a quail.)

A quail's egg: idle philosophy in solution.
(There is no wife better than a quail.)
I dropped a quail's egg into a cup for buckwheat noodles,

And made havoc of the Democratic Constitution.
Split chopsticks stuck in the back, a quail husband
Will deliver dishes on a bicycle, anywhere.

The light yellow legs go up the hill of Golgotha.
Those quails who stood on the rock, became the rock!
The nightfall is quiet, but inside the congealed exuviae

Numberless insects zigzag, on parade.

HORSE

Young girls bloom like flowers.
Unharnessed, a horse trots
Round its driver who
Grasps it by a rope.

Far off a horse is going round and round
In a square plot.

Not miserable, not cheerful either,
The bay horse is prancing,
Shaking its head, throwing up its legs
By turn: it is not running.

But there are no spectators
In what looks like an amphitheater.

White cherry petals fall like snowflakes
In the wind. All at once,
Houses, people vanish, into silence.
Nothing moves. Streetcars, buses, are held back
Silently. Quiet, everything.
All visible things become this nothingness.

The horse's bones—beautiful in their gray sheen.

A horse is going round and round,
Dancing now, with *joie de vivre,*
Under the cliff of death.

COLLAPSE

Time oozed from my pores,
Drinking tea
I tasted the seven seas.

I saw in the mist formed
Around me
The fatal chrysanthemum, myself.

Its scent choked, and as I
Rose, squaring
My shoulders, the earth collapsed.

SUN

Stretched in the genial sun
The mountain snake
Tickled its length along the rock.

The wind rustled the sunshine,
But the snake,
Fully uncoiled, was calm.

Fifty thousand years ago!
Later the same sun
Blazed across the pyramids,

Now it warms my chest.
But below, through
Shattered rock, the snake

Thrusts up its snout, fangs
Flicking at my thoughts
Strewn about the rocks like violets.

It's you, faces cut like triangles,
Have kept the snake alive!
The pavement's greened with leaves.

WORDS

I don't take your words
Merely as words.
Far from it.

I listen
To what makes you talk—
Whatever that is—
And me listen.

RAIN

The rain keeps falling,
Even in dreams.
The skull leaks badly.

There's a constant dripping
Down the back.
The rain, which no one

Remembers starting,
Keeps falling,
Even on the finest days.

BREAM

What's land? What's water?
In the window of the florist
Swims the big-eyed bream,
Between dahlias, chrysanthemums.

So you're alone? Well, forget
Others, keep talking to yourself.
Past the hydrangea leaves
Sways the scaly bream-mass.

History? Look between
The dry leaves of the sardine
Paper. Oops! the anemone's
Finally snagged a scale,

And flowering on a tulip stem,
The bream's tail and fin!
Why fear? What do you know
Of what happens after death?

Just remember to pierce
The cactus through your Christmas hat.
Brushed by trumpet lilies, roses,
The bream opens/shuts his mouth.

THE POSITION OF THE SPARROW

The sparrow has cut the day in half:
Afternoons—yesterday's, the day after tomorrow's—
Layer the white wall.
Those of last year, and next year's too,
Are dyed into the wall—see them?—
And should the wall come down,
Why, those afternoons will remain,
Glimmering, just as they are, through time.
(That was a colorless realm where,
Nevertheless, most any color could well up.)

Just as the swan becomes a crow,
So everything improves—everything:
No evil *can* persist, and as to things,
Why, nothing is unchangeable.
The squirrel, for instance, is on the tray,
Buffalos lumber through African brush,
The snail wends along the wall,
Leaving a silver trail.
The sparrow's bill grips a pomegranate seed:
Just anything can resemble a lens, or a squirrel.

Because the whole is part, there's not a whole,
Anywhere, that is not part.
And all those happenings a billion years ago,
Are happening now, all around us: time.
Indeed this morning the sparrow hopped about
In that nebulous whirlpool
A million light years hence.
And since the morning is void,
Anything can be. Since mornings
A billion years from now are nothingness,
We can behold them.
The sparrow stirs,
The universe moves slightly.

DECK

If time is but a stream flowing from past to future,
Why, it's nothing more than sardine guts!
If all is carried away by it,
Then everything is seaweed along a desolate strand!
Has this stream no end at all?
Then there ought to be an unmapped sea around it.

The tide moves at its own sweet will,
Yet whether it moves or not—who cares?
Still, an absolutely immobile ship is by the quay:
Should its anchor drop to the depths of time,
We'll have had it, the harbor will dry up.

A sailor goes ashore, walking along
With existence in the palm of his hand.
With nothing under him,
His tapering toes extend,
Then—like a meteor—disappear.

The sailor is free to go anywhere,
No deck is bigger than his hand.

MASCOT

Somebody is breathing inside me—
Birds, the very earth.

The ocean's in my chest. Walking,
I always throw myself down.

Newssheets, a puppy were dancing in the wind—
Trucks rushed by,

Empty trucks stout enough to carry the earth
On their puncture-proof tires.

The instant I raised my hand to wave,
I was nowhere.

The puppy was sprawled out on its belly,
Run over—again, again.

You're a badger, I'll bet, posing as a mascot
With that moonlit tie

And, sticking from your pocket, night's flower.

STITCHES

My wife is always knitting, knitting:
Not that I watch her,
Not that I know what she thinks.

(Awake till dawn
I drowned in your eyes—
I must be dead:
Perhaps it's the mind that stirs.)

With that bamboo needle
She knits all space, piece by piece,
Hastily hauling time in.

Brass-cold, exhausted,
She drops into bed and,
Breathing calmly, falls asleep.

Her dream must be deepening,
Her knitting coming loose.

SNAIL

The snail crawls over blackness.

Just now, in the garden,
A solid lump of snow
Slipped from the zinc roof
To behead the nandin.

Make it snappy!

In full view a stalk has been
Torn off:
Let the wind rage over the earth,
He is unaware.

His head flies to the end
Of the world,
His body is tossed
Into the ash can.

Could it be that he's the falling snow?

FISH

I hold a newspaper, reading.
Suddenly my hands become cow ears,
Then turn into Pusan, the South Korean port.

Lying on a mat
Spread on the bankside stones,
I fell asleep.
But a willow leaf, breeze-stirred,
Brushed my ear.
I remained just as I was,
Near the murmurous water.

When young there was a girl
Who became a fish for me.
Whenever I wanted fish
Broiled in salt, I'd summon her.
She'd get down on her stomach
To be sun-cooked on the stones.
And she was always ready!

Alas, she no longer comes to me.
An old benighted drake,
I hobble homeward.
But look, my drake feet become horse hoofs!
Now they drop off
And, stretching marvelously,
Become the tracks of the Tokaido Railway Line.

BODY

My body's been torn to pieces,
Limbs sway in the wind
Like those of the persimmon,
Thick with blue leaves.

Suddenly a butterfly,
My eyeballs spots
On its wings,
Takes off, brilliant.

Future's circled by a crumbling
Earthen wall, and the dog's
Pregnant with earth,
Nipples of its swollen teats

Sharp as lead in a red pencil.
As I rushed through flame
An airplane passed between
My legs. Sky's my body.

AFTERIMAGES

The volcanic smoke of Mount Aso
Drifted across the sea, white ash
Clinging to mulberry leaves
And crowning the heads of sparrows.

An open-mouthed lava crocodile;
A sparrow like a fossil sprig,
The moon filling its eyes;
A colossal water lizard stuck to a dead tree,
Its headland tail quaking.

A cloud floats in my head—beautiful!
When the sparrow opens its eyes,
Nothing but rosy space. All else gone.

Don't tell me that tree was red—
The only thing that moved, ever closer,
Was a girl's nose. All mere afterimages.

Water, coldness itself, flows underfoot.

The sparrow, eyes half closed, lay in an urn
In the pit. Now it fans up. The earth's
Fiery column is nearly extinguished.

Part V

Awakening (1973)

AWAKENING

Homage To Hakuin, Zen Master, 1685–1768

I

Shoichi brushed the black
on thick.
His circle held a poem
like buds
above a flowering bowl.

Since the moment of my
pointing,
this bowl, an "earth device,"
holds
nothing but the dawn.

II

A freeze last night, the window's
laced ice flowers, a meadow drifting
from the glacier's side. I think of Hakuin:

"Freezing in an icefield, stretched
thousands of miles in all directions,
I was alone, transparent, and could not move."

Legs cramped, mind pointing
like a torch, I cannot see beyond
the frost, out nor in. And do not move.

III

I balance the round stone
    in my palm,
turn it full circle,

slowly, in the late sun,
       spring to now.
Severe compression,

like a troubled head,
       stings my hand.
It falls. A small dust rises.

IV

Beyond the sycamore
dark air moves
westward—

smoke, cloud, something
wanting a name.
Across the window,

my gathered breath,
I trace
a simple word.

V

My daughter gathers shells
where thirty years before
I'd turned them over, marveling.

I take them from her,
make, at her command,
the universe. Hands clasped,

marking the limits of
a world, we watch till sundown
planets whirling in the sand.

VI

Softness everywhere,
snow a smear,
air a gray sack.

Time. Place. Thing.
Felt between
skin and bone, flesh.

VII

I write in the dark again,
rather by dusk-light,
and what I love about

this hour is the way the trees
are taken, one by one,
into the great wash of darkness.

At this hour I am always happy,
ready to be taken myself,
fully aware.

AWAY

Here I go again,
want to be somewhere else—
feet tramping under the desk,

I study travel brochures,
imagine monastic Hiltons,
the caravansary of my past.

Apples, cheese, a hunk of bread,
the road: what'll it be today?
I ask myself: the Seine,

Isfahan bazaar, three claps
of the hand, and Yamaguchi,
Takayama-roshi shouting—

Down, down, and breathe!
My feet go faster faster,
suddenly fly off.

Calm, breathing slowly,
I bow to Master Takayama
who smiles all the way from Japan.

MUSEUM GUARDS (LONDON)

I

He smokes against the wall
blowing rings where Moore's giants
escape through the holes

in themselves. He is small among
them, and his cigarette, the one
live thing, fizzles in the rain.

II

You would have understood what made
the guard leap from his chair
and, pointing at your saints,

cry out in Italian—
"What am I doing here?" Carlo Crivelli,
what is wrong with this world?

III

He watches us watching, weary,
cough straightening his slouch.
Seven years facing the Watteaus.

Life's no picnic. Ask him, the crippled
one who used to whisper shyly
that he was an artist, waiting for the break.

HYDE PARK SUNDAY

Suddenly the bronzed Spaniard,
yellow bandanna on his forehead,
left his companions with a leap—
perfect somersault—then cartwheeled
past the lovers on the grass.

The sprawlers gaped, on Speakers' Corner
there was silence, those angry men
turned blessed, forgiving—
so much pure energy expended for nothing,
for absolutely nothing.

ELEGY FOR A LONG-HAIRED STUDENT

He called at four a.m.: about to fly
to Mao, he had to know the Chinese word
for peace. Next day he was dead.

"Such dreams were bound for madness,"
I told his mourners. "He was too good
for this world." "He would have wanted you,"

they said. "*You* understood." Bearing
his body to the grave, I saw the long red hair
he could not stop from coiling round

their throats: Elks, Legionnaires.
Unmocked now, it would grow. As we lay
him down, I spoke that word for peace.

SOUTH

Walking at night, I always return to
        the spot beyond
the cannery and cornfields where

a farmhouse faces south among tall trees.
        I dream a life
there for myself, everything happening

in an upper room: reading in sunlight,
        talk, over wine,
with a friend, long midnight poems swept

with stars and a moon. And nothing
        being savaged,
anywhere. Having my fill of that life,

I imagine a path leading south
        through corn and wheat,
to the Gulf of Mexico! I walk

each night in practice for that walk.

NOON REPORT

Though yesterday, as forecast,
shot by on a wind
from the northwest,
promising nothing much,

this afternoon the blue
limbs of the sky
hang still. Up there,
as usual, something's

concocting tomorrow
which, despite the mess
we're bound to make of it,
should arrive on time.

CONFESSION

When with my stuffed beginner's hook
    lodged in his lip
the small-mouth bass shot up
and almost ditched the rowboat, I jerked
    the flyrod high.

Caught there, eye to eye, we flashed
    together in
the sun, flyrod ablaze
between us—midspace, midlife—
    then the plunging.

I dream him down there still,
    crawdad sucked to
bone, flyrod clicking on the lakebed
where, shrunk from the anchored hulls,
    he slowly spins.

FISHING WITH MY DAUGHTER IN MILLER'S MEADOW

You follow, dress held high above
    the fresh manure,
missing your doll, scolding Miller's horses

for being no gentlemen where they graze
    in morning sun.
You want the river, quick, I promised you back there,

and all those fish. I point to trees where
    water rides low
banks, slopping over in the spring,

and pull you from barbed wire protecting corn
    the size of you
and gaining fast on me. To get you in the meadow

I hold the wire high, spanning a hand across
    your freckled back.
At last we make the river, skimmed with flies,

you help me scoop for bait. I give you time
    to run away,
then drop the hook. It's fish I think

I'm after, you I almost catch, in up to knees,
    sipping minnowy
water. Well, I hadn't hoped for more.

Going back, you heap the creel with phlox and marigolds.

STORM

The green horse of the tree
bucks in the wind
as lightning hits beyond.
We will ride it out together,
or together fall.

AFTER THE STORM

Slick of water on
the picnic table,
beaded lawnchairs,

street steaming in
the early heat.
Thrumming underground,

dead grass will spring
again. Half way up
the maple's trunk

the first-born squirrel's
nose. The bluejay,
like a startled eye,

darts from branch to branch.

TWISTER

Waiting the twister which touched down
a county north, leveled a swath
of homes, taking twenty lives,

we sit in battered chairs, southwest
corner of the basement, listen
to the radio warnings through

linoleum and creaky floorboards
of the kitchen overhead. We are
like children in a spooky film,

ghosts about to enter at the door.
I try to comfort them, though
most afraid, *Survival Handbook*

open on my lap. Around our
piled up junk cobwebs sagged with flies,
though early spring. A trunk with French Line

stickers, paint flaked in our defective
furnace heat, a stack of dishes
judged too vulgar for our guests,

sled with rusted runners, cockeyed pram
and broken dolls, Christmas trinkets
we may use again, some boards kept

mainly for the nails. I watch my wife,
son, daughter, wondering what we're up to,
what's ahead. We listen, ever

silent, for the roar out of the west,
whatever's zeroing in with terror
in its wake. The all-clear sounds,

a pop song hits above. Made it
once again. We shove the chairs
against the wall, climb into the light.

THE CHERRY

February: the season grips—
        heavy—the chomped
stalks in Miller's field
        across the way.

Wind comes level, spurred by
        western counties,
and horses our daughter watched
        all summer long

shiver in woodland now. Below,
        piled branches
downed by the storm of mid-December
        shift in the gusts.

We have waited a month for the city
        to cart them off—
it's been so cold the ice that
        let the storm strip

clean, has scarcely thawed. The day
        those branches split
I had to axe the cherry to its roots.
        Our girl, sulking

out of range, held tight to twigs.

HERE AND NOW

Sunglasses upturned
on the picnic table,
where I try to write,

catch my reflection
square—sweaty, vain.
What's the use?

Hear a knocking
at the front. No muse,
a salesman

from the Alcoa
Aluminum Company
inspired by the siding

of our rented house.

MORNING

I lie late where
sunlight floods the curtain,
tracing dust lines here and there.

I want to remain
floating on the sheet,
a whitecap bearing me to shores I need,

a chosen world
where no one waits
and nothing cares. Soon I shall draw

the curtain
on the window tree,
quick birds among the leaf-trace.

They build around
me, everything waits
to happen. The paper on the desk

is like a distant
sunlit pool, my pen
an indolent bather, weary of all.

BLACK PARTRIDGE WOODS, BEFORE
A READING

Soon words, words, words, now silence
    in the woods
of this blue-collar town.

Noon. A freight rocks rails
    lumbering
toward Chicago. Factory whistles,

everywhere, at once. Where is
    the poet
who named these woods? Mud on my shoes,

lost for an hour with the children
    of Lemont,
Illinois, I talk of partridges and poems.

HEAT

Hundred degrees.
After four days
we are the sprawling
dead. The fingers

of the fan can't
claw through heat
piled up like earth.
Garbage steams

and buzzes—a page
from Dante's Hell.
Air burns the tips
of maple leaves.

Where's the rainmaker?
Somewhere black
clouds must form—
then why not here?

SUMMER

My neighbor frets about his lawn,
and he has reasons—
dandelions, crabgrass, a passing dog.

He scowls up at my maple, rake
clogged and trembling,
as its seeds spin down—

not angels, moths, but paratroopers
carried by the wind,
planting barricades along his eaves.

He's on the ladder now, scaring
the nibbling squirrels,
scattering starlings with his water hose.

Thank God his aim is bad
or he'd have drowned
or B-B gunned the lot. Now he

shakes a fist of seeds at me
where I sit poeming
my dandelions, crabgrass and a passing dog.

I like my neighbor, in his way
he cares for me. Look what
I've given him—something to feel superior to.

NO HITTER

By the seventh it was more than a ballgame,
I crushed the rosin-bag before each pitch.

Something said: this is it, either you make
it or you don't, all life long. Either they

hit you, or you get it by them, clean.
But they were there to do the same: either they

hit me or they don't. And it would last forever.
Balanced till the bottom of the ninth, we

grimly learned the score. Whoever pitied whom,
they hit me—my no-hitter was a route.

It was relief I felt (and got)—that power
would have scared, or so I told myself.

WHITE CITY

High on abandoned
rollercoaster tracks,
over Chicago,
a kite-tail in the wind,
we inched along the rotted
slats, proving ourselves
against the tug of earth.

Rivals' stones whizzing
by our ears, this was no
King-of-the-Mountain game,
we knew, as later on our knees
we worked our way below
with nothing in our hands,
not even stones.

MY DAUGHTER'S AQUARIUM

You ask another question,
to be put off again, then
    walk away

so sad, I call you back.
It started out with birth—
    why? how? when?

From there, promised you
would hardly burst when
    that time came,

you moved on to greater perils—
beauty vanished, friends who
    always hurt.

All, things answerable, things
assurance turned to good. And
    now you're off

again, quickly from tank
to tank, passing the porpoise
    suspended

like a plastic Disney toy,
on the edge of tears,
    hating my

half answers to your questions,
blaming me as fish dart
    from your grasp.

I follow, then pull you out
into the autumn day when
    suddenly

you want to be in water,
threaten, above sobs, to
    swim away.

THE UNKNOWN NEIGHBOR

The road you took to death
I traveled on, three hours before,
and made it safely home.

I hadn't met you, being me,
but often saw you home
from work, circled by kids

shrieking as you tossed
them up, again, again,
your wife tall in the doorway,

almost too tired to smile.
You were the perfect neighbor—
lawn mowing, leaf raking,

unborrowing—just so for
our town. And now your door
is shut, your family gone

five months since your death
to another husband, father.
Leaves pile high on lawn

and sidewalk, still throughout
the neighborhood fly rumors
of a widow's nights.

THE DUCKPOND

I

Crocus, daffodil:
  already the pond's
    clear of ice

where, winter long,
  ducks and gulls
    slid for crusts.

People circle—
  pale, bronchitic,
    jostling behind dogs,

grope toward lawnchairs
  spread like islands
    on the grass.

Sunk there, they lift faces to the sun.

II

Good Friday.
  Ducks carry on,
    a day like any other.

Same old story:
  no one seems to care.
    A loudmouth

leader of a mangy host
  spiked to a cross,
    as blackbirds in certain

lands neighboring on
  that history are splayed
    on fences, warning

to their kind. A duck soars from the reeds.

III

Man and woman
  argue past the duckpond,
    his arms flaying,

she, head down—even
  by the fully budded
    cherry, clustered

lilac boughs. Not once
  do they forget
    their bitterness,

face the gift of morning
  ducks wake to
    in the reeds.

They have things to settle, and they will.

IV

On my favorite
  bench beside the roses
    I watch ducks

smoothing feathers,
    breathing it all in.
        Catching the headline

where the bird flits
    I'm reminded
        three men were shot up

at the moon. I turn
    back to the roses:
        what

if they don't make it? If they do?

V

Lying near the pond
    in fear of the stray
        dog that daily

roams the park,
    ducks know
        their limitations,

and the world's—
    how long it takes,
        precisely,

to escape the paw thrusts
    of the dog,
        who once again

swings round to chase his tail.

VI

Radio tower
    beyond the blossoms,
        ducks

here in the pond,
    a connection
        between them—

how did I discover
    this, and why?
        Was it

the blue air? The bench
    moves beneath
        us like a seesaw,

the pond sends news of the world.

VII

What becomes of things
    we make or do?
        The Japanese lantern

or from across the pond
    beneath the trees
        a drift

of voices cultured
    and remote: water
        will carry anything

that floats. The lantern
    maker, the couple
        chatting there

would be amazed to find themselves a poem.

VIII

When tail wagging
　　　in the breeze
　　　　　the duck pokes

bill into the pondbed,
　　　keeps it there,
　　　　　my daughter thinks

him fun—he is, yet how to say
　　　those acrobatics
　　　　　aren't meant

to jollify the day. He's
　　　hungry, poking
　　　　　away at nothing

for crumbs we failed to bring: how to tell her?

IX

Ducks lie close together
　　　in morning dew, wary-eyed,
　　　　　bills pointing at the pond:

roused by squirrels,
　　　those early risers,
　　　　　air's a-whir with wings.

Sad to think of leaving
　　　this place. A helicopter
　　　　　with mysterious purpose

appears above the trees,
　　　moving low. Its circles
　　　　　tightening,

the ducks cling to the pondedge, right to fear.

THE EDGE

Living that year at the edge
of the ravine,
sloped down to the woods, we listened

to the animals before the town
awoke, blurring
the limits of our days,

forcing its round, the needs
of others.
Near sleep, after loving, we felt

part of a stillness with the dark
and all its creatures,
holding to the edge of where we lived.

FOR HELEN

You chip a tooth, complain
of getting old.
Well, I've felt old for years.

"You're as old
as you are,"
I quip and parry frowns.

"Look, we're in this
together"—that
never fails, you're in

my arms and young. Warmth
to warmth, we're
bound to last forever.

MAP

I unfold it on the desk
to trace you once again.
Though cut off by a smudge

of mountains, ropes
of water stretched between,
how easily I spread a hand

across the space that separates.
But this
cramped sheet, while true,

does not tell all. What of
that span no map will ever
show, sharper for being unseen?

THE WRITER'S WIFE

Deep in your northwood's fastness,
snowbound half the year, you complain,

he tells me, of problems with the stove,
dirt, loneliness, yet says he's proud

of your tenacity, your faith in him.
Meanwhile he writes what only you will read.

No one else would do this for him,
he whose work has come to nothing.

AMPUTEE

Something kept the blood from
going round—
he gave up one leg like a prize,

and then the other. Soon it would
be his arms.
He called it an "unwilling heart."

Jollying nurses, once he rocked
the ward with—
"Who's for football?" from his bedpan throne.

When he was readied for the saw again,
we wished him
well. He waved his bandaged hand:

"Now you see it, now you don't,"
he quipped. They
told us he died laughing under gas.

BOSTON

South Station, very early, and
come to read midwestern poems
at Tufts, due in an hour, seedy

in my all-night-slept-in suit,
I need a shave. The john of Savarin's
is full. I try the public one.

A bum is scraping skin off
at the mirror. I stand behind him,
fumble for the switch, lift

my cordless shaver to the jaw.
The tatooed stripper on his arm
begins to bump. Soap drips bloody

from his straightedge. "Give it here,"
he mutters. Razor plowing down,
I know he means it, hand

it to him, juice full on,
grab my suitcase, then half shaved
move off to read those poems.

THE EXCHANGE

As I turned from the bar,
my back to him,
he beat it through the door
with every cent I had.

"Happens everyday," the barkeep
said. I burned for weeks,
imagined trapping him
in alleyways, fists ready.

Then his face lost focus,
I found myself remembering
the tip he gave me
on a horse, his winning manner

and his guts. I'd learned
at some expense
a truth about myself,
and was twice robbed.

THE LOSER

He's there outside again, holding up
the tavern wall, whatever the day.

Never completely under—cadging,
wheedling through his tale. Few seem

to pity him. Others remember the girl
who ditched him for a carnival,

and promised she'd be back. So his
long wait began. Well, someone had to hurt,

and he was chosen: town drunk, town loser,
plastered with the ads against the wall.

CLOWN

Brush in hand, blinking
            under
                  a sombrero of whitewash,

he's shoved feetfirst
            into
                  the cannon's mouth.

Drum pointing in their chests
            children
                  hold their ears.

It's no surprise to them
            that,
                  blast still ringing,

he hits the net and springs up
            bloodless,
                  on his toes.

THE LAST ROMANTIC

"Le Duc" we hailed him to his pinched
Napoleonic face, behind
the frail brushed back, "Le Fou."

All day he'd prowl the boulevards,
gilt cane ticking, for Insult,
and when he found it, up went cane

and swish! another passer-by'd
be sliced and stacked like sausage
on the dark shelf of his mind.

Thus Le Duc until that chilly
afternoon at Jean's Café.
There he perched, like a hawk, for

Slight. The tourist hardly stopped
to gawk inside: more than enough.
"Crapaud!" Le Duc arose and charged—

what a shattering of pride!
Before they shrove him of Jean's
windowglass, Le poor Fou died.

TO ROGER BLIN

My shaky French, my coarse
Bohemian ways,
must have amused you—

you who had the "mark,"
the fiery
haunted look of postwar Paris.

Sweating over poems
in a drab
leftbank hotel, I fantasized

your life, slowly to feel
as you directed
Lorca's plays, myself

upon that stage. Was it
a style, warm
and yet severe, an honesty?

Now opening Genet's *Letters
to Roger Blin,*
I feel ashamed. I asked

too much of you: a path,
a way, the art
to make life possible.

DEAN DIXON, WELCOME HOME

Weary of their praise—"those
black expressive hands,"
tired of saying Brahms

not Gershwin was your man,
you left behind do-gooders
and their scented wives,

sailed from their "Negro Firsts"
to prove you had the gift.
Now, tall before the orchestra,

drawing urgent chords, you raise
those hands again. Times
are changed, they say, and someone

needs what you alone can give.
Seasons late, you're
welcomed home, Dean Dixon, friend.

BUSKER

Facing the playhouse queue,
straining through songs

all can remember, she muffs
a high note at the end.

As we start to shuffle in,
she scrambles for the loot.

Fat, seedy—never mind—
she is so purely what she is

no actor could do more.
Leaving the queue, I follow

her all night, hands full of coins,
songs ringing everywhere.

CHURCH CONCERT (LONDON)

Juan Arrau, guitarist, your Frescobaldi,
    Albeniz,
stir the crowded aisles of Saint Martin's,

warm the shivering woman, feet tapping
    on the pew,
and the man dozing against a pillar looks

wildly where the stained glass shatters in
    the priest's eyes.
You pierce them with a deep song from your

native South—the rush of sea, waves like
    horns against
a wall. The audience set free, Trafalgar Square

will never be the same—Nelson like
    a prowhead,
adrift once more upon the Spanish Main.

KEATS HOUSE

I sign the guest book
where some wit scrawled—
"Keats had a sore Fanny!"

Move by books, portraits,
manuscripts, his chair.
Sad—I get the feel of him,

yet something's gone,
whatever made him write:
the girl, a nightingale,

seasons of mist, which had
their music too? Beyond
the house the Heath's

not as it was, yet cold enough
to raise that chill which
kept him in these rooms, a poet

and a dying man, to do the work.

AT SHAKESPEARE'S TOMB

Tickets trailing from their fists, whispering
      about the need
      to patch, renew,
the priests take our money, lead us where

you lie boxed in beneath your likeness.
      Outside the Avon
      active with
detergent, crested here and there by dizzy swans.

Along the banks your worshippers vision you
      wading, fishing,
      rushing past them
with a mate, poached deer on shouldered pole.

Naughty, you charm them, as in the playhouse
      down the river
      you'll amaze.
In spite of Lear you have become an industry:

ten fleets of bus, fifteen Chinese cooks,
      five Italian,
      a pox of
Ye Olde this and that, guides in your father's

and your daughter's houses—possibly
        your trundle bed,
        likely your
chamberpot. Tourists, cameras weighing

down their heads, seize you at last. Meanwhile
        a grateful bed-
        and-breakfast town
rejoices in your power, its poetry.

SNIPER

        An inch to the left
        and I'd be twenty years
        of dust by now. I can't

        walk under trees without
        his muzzle tracks me.
        He'd hit through branches,

        leaves pinned to his shoulders
        whistling. We searched him
        everywhere—up trunks,

        in caves, down pits. Then
        one night, his island taken,
        he stepped from jungle

        shade, leaves still pinned
        upon him glistening
        in the projector's light,

        and tiptoed round to watch
        our show, a weary kid
        strayed in from trick-or-treat.

FORWARD OBSERVERS

Our lensed hill-splitting eyes
useless in the dark, they
flanked us through the night.

Indispensable, we called
down thunder from the hills,
and saved a thousand.

Each of us worth, some claimed,
one hundred men,
they needed yet despised us.

Their bodies held like sandbags.
We survived,
part of something coming, vile as war.

THOROUGHBRED COUNTRY

Lexington to Louisville: the Greyhound
moves through bluegrass, the stud, its mares,
caught delicately on the soft hill.

It's all horse talk past Calumet,
"richest acres" in the world.
Blue—the grass, the sky, the blood.

Conscripts in the bus, straight
from the hollows, first time away,
are wondering what awaits them.

A black horse gallops from the shadows.
The young men look away.
No one speaks until we enter Louisville.

EVENING

Weary, I seek relief behind
the paper, before the set
where they emerge, the victims,

through walls and floorboards,
summoning to a ritual
hung with fear, myself enacted,

inflicting and inflicted pain.
From fissures in the earth,
from smoking thatch they rush

toward me, arms like torches,
children grasped between,
cries hurtling oceans meant

to separate. What can I do?
Put down, switch off—
plunge to the barricades of sleep.

SUNDAY. THE BELLS.

All over town they
rise from beds,
heavy with dreams
of sons dying in Viet Nam.

Sunday. The bells ring
in the terrible emptiness
of bedrooms their distant
sons dream girls into.

LETTER TO JEAN-PAUL BAUDOT, AT
CHRISTMAS

Friend, on this sunny day, snow sparkling
everywhere, I think of you once more,
how many years ago, a child Resistance

fighter trapped by Nazis in a cave
with fifteen others, left to die, you became
a cannibal. Saved by Americans,

the taste of a dead comrade's flesh foul
in your mouth, you fell onto the snow
of the Haute Savoie and gorged to purge yourself,

somehow to start again. Each winter since
you were reminded, vomiting for days.
Each winter since you told me at the Mabillon,

I see you on the first snow of the year
spreadeagled, face buried in that stench.
I write once more, Jean-Paul, though you don't

answer, because I must: today men do far worse.
Yours in hope of peace, for all of us,
before the coming of another snow.

Part VI

From *Selected Poems* (1976)

THE FACE

Weekly at the start
of the documentary
on World War II

a boy's face, doomed,
sharply beautiful,
floats in the screen,

a dark balloon
above a field of barbs,
the stench of gas.

Whoever holds the
string
will not let go.

RAIN

Lazy afternoon, rain
drizzling down the path,
soft hum of my daughter

and her friends: moments
of quiet, untroubling.
But now the neighbor's child

skips out in old boots,
umbrella arched, rain
sopping her blue dress.

Like a small animal
she caves against the storm:
yesterday her father caught

messing with the sitter,
today the hurried packing,
and the constant rain.

SIRENS

Someone calls for help,
always.
He called yesterday,

he will call tomorrow.
Yesterday he was on fire,
today his hand

was chewed off by the steel
teeth of a combine,
tomorrow he will lurch

from a smashed car,
take two steps, collapse
onto his red shadow.

His voice, familiar,
pierces everywhere:
it will be heard.

THE GORGE

There is something
between us
I must pass to
reach you,
hand over hand,
legs swinging,

sharp scent
of brush rising
from the gorge bed.

My arms strain
as finally
I sight you—
you
who are most
aware of the
painful art
I practice,
and for whom.

OX

Another day
    half over,
raising hoofs
    where horns
slice through
    the clouds.
Darkness
    streams down
the flanks,
    filling the
scented field,
    but somewhere
night is
    touched off
by a horn,
    columns of
light form
    under the
rippling body—
    once more
to pasture
    in my eyes.

MOLE

Hunched in the basement,
shadow on the wall,
six feet down and glad to be alive.

Overhead, wilting memory
of long dog days,
earthmovers rumble in the haze

through trees, corn, soybeans—
steel, concrete,
glass to come. I need

this burrow, cool, sunken
with roots. What
will remain, I wonder, when

I tunnel up from where I hunch,
shadow on the wall,
six feet down and glad to be alive.

I. M. PABLO PICASSO

(for my father)

All is ordinary again—
in a thousand places,
convergences,

displaced parts flying
together: an ear,
a nose, a breast spinning

like a hand-grenade,
a third eye shot
with cloud, deep, staring,

and here, in Chicago
a great
flapping of wings.

CARLO CRIVELLI: CRUCIFIXION

Sulphurous storm-
light
over Calvary.

The Sold Man
yellowing
under thorns,

feet caked with
stations
of the cross.

Soon a blossoming
from
the cairn:

those hooded
stones
will split.

SNOW

Centuries
snow
has drifted
"feather like"
through poems,
so thick,
one on a ladder,
connoisseur
of snows,
archivist
of weathers,
gingerly raising
a ten-foot pen,
climbing
after it onto
that frozen waste,
would find
much snow,
little poetry.
Meanwhile
the writer,
after many weeks,
feels
his hand move—
now it stops,
a footprint artist
pausing
in the snow.

THE GOOSE

Magnificent
against October maples
the goose
twisting in downdraft
shot to the highway,
crushed on my wheels—
I braked
wanting to rush out,
imagined
its strong arc south again.

Blaring cars
shadowed
as I started up,
driving for miles
in innocence
in guilt
not caring where I headed,
a whiteness
mangled
in the maples, everywhere.

LOVE POEM

Startle my wife again—
"Where will we lay our bones?"

Harmless, you'd think, yet
she's berserk. "Mere joshing,"

I protest. She will not
listen. I want an island

for us, apart, ringed with stones,
clusterings of flowers

merging us closer through
the all of time. She thinks

me mad with dreaming,
but it's love for her

which spurs me, this need
to know we'll never separate.

FRIENDSHIP

He writes again. Since his divorce
a fist has never left his chest.

He needs my words, and so I fill
a sheet—what joy it gives

to utter words to eyes that plead
from paper. I place the softest

on his cheek, his brow, a special one
upon his mouth. Sigh across

the page that he still has a friend.
Now off to do its loving work,

my scroll of bandages and kisses,
my dried and flattened heart.

BARBECUE

Mister and Missus
Carnalot,
friendly folk,
stoke up the fire.

His and Hers aprons
flush in the
char-smoke. They
are ablaze while

the spit turns,
rekindling ashes,
sipping, seasoning,
done to a turn.

Readying long forks,
prongs move together,
his toward Hers,
hers toward His.

SHADOW

Always coming, neat head
tilted, "Mad" Nolgate
shadows these streets for years,

surviving playground taunts,
the school's Least Likely.
Prompt as the townclock,

passes old classmates
at work, flusters wives
wilting by chain-store greens,

scattering their kids—
thunder on pavement,
storming through grass.

Let loose inside himself,
cushioned in air,
he walks on forever.

RITES OF PASSAGE

Indian river swollen brown and swift:
the pebble from my hand sounds above
    the southfield—

soybeans, corn, cicadas. Stone rings
touch the bank, ripple up my arm.
    In the grass

a worm twists in webbed air (how things
absorb each other)—on a branch
    a sparrow

tenses, gray. As grass stirs it bursts
from leaves, devouring. I close my book.
    With so much

doing everywhere, words swimming green,
why read? I see and taste silence.
    Starlings flit,

blue/black feathers raising spume
of dandelions, young fluttering
    in the twigs.

I think of my grown son who runs
and heaves me to my feet—our
        promised walk

through woods. As he pulls back a branch
hair on his forearm glistens
        like the leaves

we brush by. I follow down the path
we've loved for years. We try to
        lose ourselves,

yet there's the river, churning south.
I muse on what I've given,
        all I can't.

My son moves toward the bank, then turns.
I stop myself from grasping
        at his hand.

Part VII

New Poems (1983)

CHERRIES

Because I sit eating cherries
which I did not pick
a girl goes bad under

the elevator tracks, will
never be whole again.
Because I want the full bag,

grasping, twenty-five children
cry for food. Gorging,
I've none to offer. I want

to care, I mean to, but not
yet, a dozen cherries
rattling at the bottom of my bag.

One by one I lift them to
my mouth, slowly break
their skin—twelve nations

bleed. Because I love, because
I need cherries, I
cannot help them. My happiness,

bought cheap, must last forever.

ELM

Beetles smaller than
rice-grains hollowed
the weathered trunk,

piling sawdust high.
Fearing another storm
might axe the sparse-

leafed branches through
the shingles, I loosed
bird-feeder ropes, gave

up the elm to Shabbona
Tree Service. Watched
birds spiral, squirrels

bolt as limbs crashed
down. By afternoon, sun
warmed the jagged stump,

and the stone roof once
overhung by leaves. Season
turning, frost spiked

the twigless air. Soon
snow filled emptiness
between the shrubs. I

fed my elm-logs to the
fire, sending ghost-
blossoms to the sky.

SAVANTS

Their hour had come
and gone: notions
blueprinted, years

of infinite zeros,
halved, quartered,
atomed for this day—

test-tubes of dust
measured to shake the
world. Now it was

done. Reaming traces
from their nails,
scattering like rocks

they'd blasted from
the earth, they turned
to raking gardens,

lecturing on peace,
regrets black-signatured
across an ashen page.

Secret codes unlearnt,
they crawled back to the
past on hands and knees.

IN OUR TIME

When after the blast
they turned to the poet,
he asked for a handful
of nails. Pounded them
like phrases into old
boards. No bittersweet,
no roses now. He knelt
in silence in the wasted
town—a stain under the
fallout moon. Nails, line
by line, his only song.

WHERE WE ARE

I sit beneath the linden's
heart-spread leaves, watch

three starlings on the bird-
bath watching me. Book on

one knee, I drain my glass:
young shoots, already doomed,

thrust withering tendrils
through the clay-bogged soil.

Last night, at the May Fair,
girls in Elizabethan garb

offered a madrigal to buds
of spring. Today the neighbor's

cat stalks fledglings in the
pine. Time was I'd run him

off. Now I just sit and trust
to his bad luck. Slowly sun

tinges leaves, hazes pine
needles. A mower sputters—

cat leaps from the shade,
into the moment, where we are.

THE ORDINARY

To love the ordinary—
fifty feet of dandelions
        and burdock,

and a small house perched
on concrete under a dying
        Chinese elm.

To be content with neighbor-
banter over a crooked fence,
        days, nights, years.

And not to regret—sun
torching the willow-oak—
        some Elsewhere.

DIRGE

        Hair, weathered
        nest, shedding

        from nerve ends.
        Ears, nose, mouth:

        muting, knobbing,
        pursing into caverns

        where necessities—
        air, water, pottage—

        filter, slop. As
        eyes blur, worlds

        move further from
        the flushed beast—

        heart—pounding
        its sullen song.

I. M. EUGENIO MONTALE

The day you turned to face
the nothingness men fear—

drunken with your secret,
like the eel, "sister of

the rainbow," arcing through
seven seas—was like

any other. Poet, you needed
fear, as one needs salt

to feel the deepest wounds.
This morning, in a Milan

hospital's antiseptic chill,
you turned for the last time

to meet that void, words
drowned in waves of light.

DAWN

Five a.m., and I've been
up for hours. My lamp,
false star, holds back

the dark. In the next
room my wife guards our
closeness deep in dream.

I love this sleeplessness,
cloistered unbroken
hours over a spotless page,

the book with all the
answers on the shelf. I
doodle on one, thumb

through the other, now
and then. This hour, it
makes no difference.

I sit back, let thoughts
come as they may. Who
knows, before dawn rides

the oak across the way,
the book may jostle just a
bit, the paper bear a poem.

NOVEMBER

First frost, the blue spruce
against my window's shagged,
and the sky is sombering. I

draw close to the fire, inward
with all that breathes. This
morning, stacking firewood,

I shattered leaf-drifts by
the shed, trailing the rabbit
burrowed there. Soon we'll

be wintering, he and I, our
paths will often cross upon
the snow. I drink good

luck to both of us, he in his
sticks and leaves, and I in
mine. Summer, the neighbor

blamed his marauding for the
shrinking salad patch, hinting
the yards would be well rid

of something two dogs, even
a tent of wire could not keep
out. I muttered to myself,

dropped my carrot like a
calling card behind the shed.
Now the spruce twists slowly

into dark. I pour another
drink. Within the hour the moon
will kindle every frosted limb.

YOU MUST CHANGE YOUR LIFE

Of all things one might be:
a squirrel lopes by

busy at being himself
in a tough nutless world,

cats at his young, rain
slanting in his nest,

night falling, winter
not provided for—

no questions to ask
of himself or anyone.

WHY I WRITE

Someone years ago forced
me to learn the alphabet,
spell, form sentences
of mouth, of hand—
long streets which, on

occasion, led to resonant
spots: at one I surprised
a bluejay bickering in
a pinetree—that blue/green
flash carried me to the

next sentence, at the end
of which two lovers came
to a full stop. Thus grew
my habit: paragraphs of
wheezy cats, windbagging

crickets, children whooping
under bell-clear skies.
These days I stroll along,
casually turn corners where
someone in black collects

my lines on a white page,
then scurries off, long
scroll trailing. No idea
what he does with them.
The other day, in a small

town, on an odd shelf, I
glimpsed a book bearing
my name. Tempted to look
inside, I hurried on. I'm
really too faint-hearted.

DESK

Dictionary
Typewriter

Paper
Seven pipes

Ashtray
Three pens

Two elbows

NOMADS

(Meshed, Iran)

Yearly they descend
scorched slopes, scatter
black tents between
abandoned wells, to graze
flocks where children
tumble in the dust.
Indifferent to strangers
come to stare, shying
from their smells. Evenings,
draped in matted skins
knotted with sheep-gut,
they squat before tents,
smoke, laugh, bend above
flutes. Their women,
turning sheep-spits, recall
days of drought, when
foraging on all fours,
they scratched for tufts
with the herds. Chanting

to flute-notes, they turn turn,
far from the lives of
strangers—soft, up on
hind legs, coming, going.

THE GREAT EXCEPTION

After the inspection at the Gate
she joined the others waiting
in blue shapeless gowns for their

assignment. From the start she
felt it a mistake, but what she'd
heard here of the other place

discouraged her complaining. Silent
gazes disapproved. Maybe it was
an air acquired on the streets,

a painted scarlet letter. Alone
as always, she trailed behind
the others: reaching at last

The Spirit of the Universe, learned
to her astonishment she was the
Great Exception, chosen as an image

of her kind. She wondered what
was expected of such favor, found
it was in Heaven's interest to token

fairness—all were equal here.
Yet where was compensation in this
Paradise of inner gardens, secured

from men? Pining away a dozen years
of everlasting life, she must
revolt. Her tongue, long gentled,

found its former salt. Loosening
her gown, unpinning her hair, she
was discovered wandering naked in

archangels' quarters. For that
and other sins she was advanced,
with proclamation, to a higher

order, greatest of Great Exceptions.

EXTERMINATOR

Phone vibrates all winter. The
exterminator cringes—
yet another squeal, demanding

he come fast. He plays at cat
and mouse, stalling them hours,
days. Then pocketing thick

gloves, flashlight, steelwool,
poison, he enters musty corners,
sets dry traps, pours tempting

pellets into little paper boats,
launches them here and there.
As he stuffs holes, he contemplates

the toughness of a world which
outlaws creatures he has learned
to love: starved from frozen

corn-stripped fields, small wonder
they outsmart those who grudge them
a few crumbs, a little warmth. The

exterminator does his job, takes his
money, leaves. In the long run of
things, he knows who will survive.

THE CITY: A CYCLE

I. Calendar

Another year: curbs
strewn with Christmas
trees, tinsel floats

the thaw. We've stumbled
to the end, driven by
storms still rumbling

overhead. Earth speaks
what we already know,
in pain relearn. On

the wall the Japanese
calendar, pure of our
devisings, mists beyond

peaks, temples, pines
where we survive. Page
by page guards secrets,

as we start out again.

II. *Grant Park*

Crush of frost:
they walk sharp-eyed
the paths familiar
as their floors—

men nearing death,
our fathers, pulled
unresisting to
the center. There,

on charged corners,
they watch, chat,
doze, heads lifted
to the wind, that

bringer, taker away—
music in the welter
of their lives. Day
deepens. They rouse

from benches, shiver,
stare about, then
cautiously return.
Each to his place,

to read once more
of what the day has
brought: another
birth, another death.

III. *Downtown*

He is the one their laws
are made for—
speeder drunkard despoiler

of daughters. Born for
tar and feathers, he stalks
in shadow. In shops his

is the dollar held up to
the light. Threatened
by factory whistles, slying

from work, he's first for
welfare. Nightly thanks city-
hall with chalked graffiti:

mayor policechief judge.

IV.   *Lake Dawn*

Slow spread of light
beyond the tracks,
fingering bare branches

of the oak. After
thick year on year
another chance to find

what dawn, rising on
frosty air, will
bring. Yesterday, ice

floes on the lake, a
revelation: nothing's
warmer than sun-webbed

snow, boots scorching
on the crust. What
will I learn today?

I thirsted seasons,
dragging a leaden shadow
into nothingness. Now,

as fire meets ice, I see.

V. *City Spring*

There's a slow
twisting underground,
as if a giant,

winter long buried
under ice,
clutching roots,

now turns face-up,
stirring the
ancient sexual play:

everywhere his warm
flesh touches—
green, yellow, red.

VI. *The Beach*

Winds over the city,
where once, fanned by

bird-wings, we strolled
the lake-edge. Now

cars and factories fume
every breathing thing,

blacken trees, speckle
flowers, blight grass,

fill lungs of children
leap-frogging on the

sand. They stop their play
to wonder as, fins spread,

mouths agape, dead alewives
float in with the tide.

VII.   *Monarchs*

A shower of spotted
wings, Monarchs drift
by factory gates,
settling in trees.

Steel beats for miles.
How fresh, early autumn
gusts that teeter
branches as they cling.

Easy to mistake them,
clustered in the pine,
for blazing cones. Thus
they outwit the starlings

wheeling by. Lassitude,
soft giving up, has
stilled their wings,
summer folds behind them.

VIII.   *Winter Storm*

Bitter night. The westwind
blasts us from our moorings.
Beyond, sends towns like drunken
boats over five hundred miles

of frozen fields. Sirens, which
all night foretold, the radio
which echoed, whimpering, have
given up, and now the city is

the wind's. We're left to our
devices. Fifteen below, the
storm has just begun. A
sputtering gas-jet, shrinking

candle keep us from perishing,
as we watch through whirled
trees a sky scorched with stars.
Sleepless, we pace room to room,

waiting the dawn. Know there
are those for whom dawn never
came, worlds that storms wiped
out before, and storms to come.

IX.   *Chicago Christmas*

Midday, watch the stranger
inching down the icy street. Last
night we opened presents by
the fire, ate, drank one toast
after another. Flames crackled,

reeled with our contentment.
Now we return to selves, peace
settling like ash. Grab my
duffle, head down to the lake,
tramp snow, knee-high, across

the bridge, air stinging nose
and eyes. Soon ice will melt.
Somewhere this water flows
tides will batter shores where
hunger's in the wind. Tomorrow

left-overs of feasts will drip
from garbage trucks, tinseled
trees strew curbs of houses
street on street, and wonderment
of pampered children dim. As

sun dips behind glazed rooftops,
imagine scrawling across twilight—
"Live as if this day will never
end." Recross the bridge,
back to whatever's left of joy.

THERE ARE DAYS

Days when speech won't come,
there's pain in words.

To utter nothings:
it's raining, there's the sun.

Not caring less but more,
how hard the language

of consent. It's in
the deeps of silence,

hour on hour, I feel
grains, stones, trace

names of all I lack.
Then suddenly

hear train whistles,
possibilities,

return, surprised, to
fragments of myself.

THE WORD

How inadequate words are
to all we know and feel—

Love Justice Honor Truth—
each emptier than the other.

If there were one word, not
spun of cloud but struck

from stone, a sudden cry,
brief, mighty, to show us as

we really are, small, cruel,
it would to our amazement

gather, merge into a final
tongue, echoing years—

the silence that would follow
prepare us for the world.

SOUL

Often evoked, exalted,
the soul might crouch
for years between

breastbone, esophagus,
conscience in a cage,
buzzing the ears,

pulling firm strings
behind eyes, patching up
heart-sores with cloudy

visions. My soul just
sits here, out of
action, arms wrapped

around stiffening knees,
sour looks on its
once friendly face.

I resent its power,
the scorn for all I write—
wrung from dreams it

feeds me, now and then.

ELLWOOD HOUSE

The carriage-way, bristling beneath
gimcrack, sends thorniest vibrations
from the house that barbs built. From
here came deft contraptions, honed

steel for cattle flanks, blocking
the cowboy's path, cutting antelope
from the most fragrant grass. The wire
piled high, each barb a dollar in

the bank. Prize objects gathered:
lacquer from the East, marble from Italy,
commode with spindly legs from France,
carved swan-cradle that rocked sons

of czars, bannister spiraling like an
oaken fence in the cathedral hall. While
the town gaped, others claimed the idea,
set up new plants. More coils rolled

out, parceling prairie miles, the West,
on through the world. They prospered:
children schooled expensively, women
scented, jeweled, gowned to divert

rich and famous. Two strands of twisted
wire cleared a cornfield for a mansion
like a sugared cake, set among weathered
silos. Enticed great chefs from Europe,

fashioned a ballroom where chanteuses,
chamber music thrilled the night.
Through war, peace, slavery, revolt
their fiddlers led the dance—

parting man from man, beast from beast.

WAKING UP IN STREATOR

I am wakened by a poem
I have never heard, in

a town never visited
deep in Illinois. Last

night, due to read poems
500 miles away—now

shaggy from dream—I
remember a friend, long dead,

who grew up in Streator,
played football, talked tough,

scorning all dreamers.
Yet one night, late,

loosened by beer, confessed
he'd once written a poem.

CONSTELLATION

Behind the super-
market where we
forage for our

lives, beyond the
parking lot, crammed
garbage bins—

thick heads of
bee-swarmed
seed-choked

sunflowers blaze
down on me through
fogged noon air.

NODDING

Half way through the play—
Marlowe at that—
I nod off into five acts

of my own, become Edward II,
betrayed, restored, betrayed
again. Wavering, frivolous,

tossed by intrigues, I snore
away, indifferent to rumors
ravaging my throne. Dream

scene on scene, cringe as they
butcher one friend, then
another. Hunger for innocence,

whimper for peace, damn my
adulterous queen, luring
assassins to me. The book

slips from my fingers, spins
like a crown. Startled,
I rise—the play has ended.

SIBERIA

Small wood towns silvered
        by birches,
sharp blue at windows, doors.

Grimed, forgotten domes,
        a gold cross:
cows, chickens haunt the tombs.

Train lurches on: ten miles west
        of Irkutsk,
where Chekhov, bound for convict

Sakhalin, once spent a night,
        I hear three
sisters longing, Moscow, Moscow!

At the Siberian heart, concrete
        crammed with facts:
who produced what, how much, when,

in what spirit. On the
    last ruled sheet
a finger-smudge points like

a holy candle. November: in
    seven days
drums, bugles, flags will whip

town after town. On wind-
    scourged platforms
throngs mill under likenesses

of hero farmers—ribboned,
    bemedaled,
exalted by a fourth sister,

one Chekhov did not know, who
    pitying
her sisters' discontent accepted

solitude and hardship, despite
    the need, at
times unbearable, of Moscow, Moscow!

JUGGLER

Someone with skill juggles
three worlds together,
rainbow, miraculous arc.

Something compels a fourth,
widening the circle. Five,
six float in the charged

steep of his mind: soon
others whirl his wrist.
Seven, eight—now he's on

his toes, up, up, rising
with the music of the
spheres. Still unsatisfied,

risks the lot, down on his
knees. He dare not drop one.
Our lives depend on it.

EXILE'S RETURN

I've decided to return,
to show them. Any place,
too long, begins to grate.

On coming to this island,
I was treated like a
lord. As one might expect,

familiar now, I disappoint,
my image pales. Daubing
a sunset on the Western Cliff,

I hear them jeer. Turn,
catch them gawking at
my canvas. Drape the easel

with my smock, enter my hut,
refuse their dole of food.
For that my woman will not

come. First time in months,
I sleep alone. Waken
to stench outside my door—

a dead dog's rotting there.
Later, I'll pack my paints,
my few mildewed belongings,

hop the mailboat to the harbor,
make for home. Humbled,
perhaps, but far from done.

My soul is what they're after.
I'll show those ingrates up
for what they are. Brush

dipped in blood, I'll paint
a masterpiece none dare ignore.
My art will make them suffer.

SMOKE

Smoke from my briar
hovers between pages
    on my lap,

clouds thought on
thought, drifts toward
    voices in

dark suits newsmongering
another day. I
    choke the sound,

knock ashes out, tamp
fresh leaf in, light
    up again.

"Smoke!" my grandson
cries, climbing beside
    me, joyfully

grasping rings. A
moment, shielded there,
    I hold him

to me, soothing the
outrage in the hot bowl
    of my mind.

WATCHING WAR MOVIES

Always the same: watching
World War II movies on TV,
landing barges bursting onto

islands, my skin crawls—
heat, dust—the scorpion
bites again. How I deceived

myself. Certain my role would
not make me killer, my unarmed
body called down fire from

scarred hills. As life took
life, blood coursed into
one stream. I knew one day,

the madness stopped, I'd make
my pilgrimage to temples,
gardens, serene masters of

a Way which pain was bonding.
Atoms fuse, a mushroom cloud,
the movie ends. But I still

stumble under camouflage, near
books of tranquil Buddhas by the
screen. The war goes on and on.

MEMORIAL DAY

Three deliberate shots
fire this quiet town,

scatter sparrows from
the willow-oak, touch

the scar where over thirty
years ago the mortar

fragment hit: I know
once more how good it is

to live. Thinking of the
boy struck down beside

me by that shell, I see
him sink into slow jungle

green, shock burned forever
in his eyes. Again I

crawl to comfort his last
breath. Even now there's

nothing I can do but, as
the bugle fades, remember.

CHORAL

Goodby, philosophers,
sorry we didn't listen:

now we pay. You
reasoned moderation,

we chose excess.
Extolled effort, we

lazed unconcerned.
Praised wisdom,

as we scratched behinds
and yawned. Not giving

up, you warned of
barbarism, as we goose-

stepped off. Railed
at gods, who shoved us,

eyes closed, to our
knees. Did you mean

to leave us, bungling,
half alive in a world

half made, stirring
a fission-caldron?

How will we ever know?
Your tomes are laced

with worms, your statues
molder, faceless,

in abandoned squares.

MACHINES

Centuries
before reckoning,
cave walls,

stone-scratched
with birdwings,
took flight—

hurling with
flint arrows
down the black

hole of time.
Fracturing worlds,
brief puffs

of dust, metal
and bone.
Yesterday—two

planes colliding,
five hundred
wiped out.

GRIEF

Our first home, after journeying
years. Look up from my desk
through maples, spruce, sycamore

at sunrise, dusk, wonder that
this place is ours. Through
sun-fired boughs, I watch a young

man amble, zipping hunting jacket,
from the house across the way,
toss shotgun in the back seat

of his Dodge, rev up the motor,
race off for deerblood. Tonight
he lies in the funeral parlor,

lost to cries of grief. Strangers,
we visit mourners in the room
he paneled, stare in the mirror

he framed and polished to a blaze.
Confused, they wonder whose words
sent him frenzied into night to drink

with hunting buddies. Out of their
pain we trace long months of failure:
divorced father of two, returned

to them jobless, rented house
gone up in flames. Clasping our
hands, their eyes demand reasons.

We offer pity, return to our home,
shadowed by trees, ashamed we can
offer no more, for the death of a son.

THE ROSE

My love, as I lie next
to you, close against your
        pain, I begin

to understand the secret
of the rose, how always
        beneath one

petal another forms, how
none of its fragrant
    lips reveal

this joining. Thirty years
I've tried to know what holds
    me to you.

Now: deep within, beyond
what hand or eye can reach,
    the thorn

is bared against the
first impulsive thrust,
    against the last.

CLASSROOM

Achievements of T'ang
Dynasty poets pass
over the blonde girl

in the striped dress,
third row on the left.
Wretchedly, she bends

over a letter—life
overwhelms. In or
out of love, she's on

that heaviest of seas.
Wang Wei's vision fills
the room. My chalky

mutterings of mountains,
rushing winds stir
nothing in her eyes. Her

thoughts are dynasties
away, shadowed by all
her life need ever know.

EVELYN

When she phones late, I listen
for disaster. At times
the epilogues were left to me.

She vows to end her life: I
grasp the phone, shaking as
the line goes dead, fearing

the worst until she calls again.
At times I've told her firmly—"No.
No use to visit, you need help

more than consolation." That
always hurts. As teacher I listened
hours, pitied. Now she sees me

father that she never knew. Last
night she was more easy, back with
a boy who hasn't torched a building

in some time. Touched by common
need, they soothe each other in
their wretchedness. Reminded of

her gifts, of comfort in reordering
one's world, she made me guardian
of all her tortured art, so with

her end I might restore another.
It's when she probes my poems, seeking
answers to unmake her wrongs, I

most despair. She chides me when my
lines don't pacify, presses me to
change them for her sake and mine.

Recently I've fathomed, phone gripped
hard, she thinks that I'm the one
needs help. She's there to give it.

THE PARK

All summer long rednecks,
high-school dropouts rev
motorbikes and souped-up
cars across the isle of
grass, jeer at cops cruising
as the horseshoes fly.
Strollers, joggers, children
traipsing to the city pool
flinch at hoots and whistles,
radio blasts recoiling from
the trees. Autumn, as leaves

ambered over picnickers
carousing on their patch, three—
caught upending gravestones
in the cemetery close by—
said they'd no place to go

but call upon the dead.
Winter sifts still white hours.
The toughs, the dropouts,
holed up somewhere with their
beer and joints, dream of
horseshoes looping shadowy oaks.

FIREWOOD

The old Norwegian backs his pick-up
on the grass, helps stack oak
and maple, split clean for my winter
hours. As we stir a rabbit, he

tells of tramping through woods on
this very land some thirty years
before. Points, squinting, two hundred
yards toward the river, talks fast

for a farmer, amused at my pure pleasure
at the wood we pile together on the
lawn, this sharp December day. Last
log in place, he lights a cigarette,

puffs deep, muses, "Never got back
to the old country." Say I'm sorry,
speak of fjords flaming under midnight
suns. He shrugs, spits at a tree,

reasons, "Where else in the world
could I say, president's a friend of
mine?" He motions west. "When we
were boys in Dixon he went down the

cattle market with me and the old man—
had good times." "Must feel proud,"
I tell him. He asks me what I do.
Confess I teach, write poems. He

eyes me warily, climbs into his cab,
starts the motor, rolls the window down,
asks, "Did you vote for him?" I
shake my head, wave as he roars off.

I tidy around the woodpile, haul in
some logs, light up our first fire in
our first real home, sit back, relax.
Just as he said, the seasoned flames

lick high into the draft, the logs
burn slow. In spite of politics, this
is an honest deal. I'll have to make
it last. He might not come again.

OLD FOLKS HOME

Always near dusk
in the shadow of
cedars, he mourns
the loss of another

day. The empty path
winds to fields pulsing
gold, green under
vapors, rain-fresh

furrows stretching
miles. Each afternoon
the old man ambles
under branches,

remembering his farm,
wife long dead, sons
buried in lives
of their own. There

he stands hours, keen
to the cool scent
of fullness—now
without purpose where

corn-tassels blow.
Returns to the bare
room, high above cedars,
gathering gold and green.

FORTUNE TELLER

In half-light, over a cloudy ball,
mumbo-jumboing what you crave,

I, diviner of palms, trace
life, love, profit, await your

silver. Lift one hand, the other,
wonder which clamped in greed,

stole from the needy, turned down
the thumb that might have saved.

Such innocents here. Follow each
crease, trying to please, name

lines, wrinkles, seams. Whisper
the future, over and over, pretending

to find in your hand what is there
in your eyes—await your silver.

FLESH

Skin's blotched, all
night I've scratched.
Arm's become a scroll,
a deep stigmata.

Message from within:
something's giving up,
hardly worth the candle
anymore. Under my

scholar's cap, read
doom. Spread ointment
as the hooks etch
crimson. Knock back

a glass of wine, hoping
for ease. Is this
how it all ends? Eyes
dim, breath short, skin

festering? Again the
tingling, everywhere
at once. Today,
tomorrow—bear up,

best I can, to the
unbearable. Swig my
wine, slide down its
shaky rope to peace.

COSMOS

Moon, magnified 1000
times, overwhelms—

hunched on this crumb
of earth, I cringe as

tongues sum up existence
for me. Out there,

the colossus, one hand
fumbling stars, the

other whipping comets
at my back. I peer up,

breathless, rub my eyes.
From the shadow of my

smallness cry boldly at
the beauty, at the pain.

THE STRANGER

He shuffled up, sat down beside
me on the parkbench, removed his
battered hat, remarked on splendors

of a London spring, noting each
flower by name. Pointing to a twisted
pine, saw what I visioned there.

Sensed I was troubled, offered
comfort as he learned my wife was
desperately ill. Uncannily, he

drew from me my past. Then told
me of his life. Shabby philosopher,
he'd traveled everywhere, placed

my accent in midwest America. He
probed on, unraveled things no books
revealed. My son, stirring in his

carriage at my side, made me aware
of time. The stranger rose, hand
on my shoulder. Said I'd be all right,

promised we'd meet again. Years since.
My son now has a small son of his own.
Last summer, in the garden with my

wife, I watched our grandson gathering
cones beneath the pine. Dozed off.
On waking, looked up, saw the stranger

doff his battered hat, seeming well
satisfied. I started, found it
was the breeze making a moving shadow

of a twisted branch. Recalled the
stranger's promise we would meet
again. Come back, a spirit of the pine.

KANRANTEI

(Wave Pavilion)

Spilled from the pines
        of Matsushima,
crests—charged with cones
        and needles—

fray tasseled ropes circling
    rocks below
the shrine. Beyond, in
    misted reaches

of the Bay, a flawless scroll.
    Five giant
guardians of Godaido Temple
    wait on

pilgrims chanting over
    half-moon
bridges, as waves swell, break
    over Kanrantei.

WILLOWS

(for Taigan Takayama, Zen master)

I was walking where the willows
ring the pond, meaning to reflect
on each, as never before, all
twenty-seven, examine twig by twig,
leaf by pointed leaf, those delicate
tents of greens and browns. I'd

tried before, but always wound up
at my leafless bole of spine, dead
ego stick, with its ambitions,
bothers, indignations. Times
I'd reach the fifth tree before
faltering, once the seventeenth.

Then, startled by grinding teeth,
sharp nails in the palm, turn back,
try again. Hoping this time to
focus on each bough, twig, leaf,
cast out all doubts that brought
me to the willows. This time

it would be different, could see
leaves shower from the farthest
tree, crown my head, bless my eyes,
when I awakened to the fact—
mind drifting to the trees ahead.
I was at fault again, stumbling to

the flap of duck, goose, a limping
footstep on the path behind,
sun-flash on the pond. Such excuse,
easy to find, whether by willows
or bristling stations of a life.
Once more, I'm off. This time

all's still. Alone, no one to blame
distractions on but self. Turn in
my tracks, back to the starting point.
Clench, unclench my hands, breathe in,
move off telling the leaves like
rosary-beads, willow to willow. Mind

clear, eye seeing all, and nothing.
By the fifth, leaves open to me,
touch my face. My gaze, in wonderment,
brushes the water. By the seventh,
know I've failed. Weeks now, I've been
practicing on my bushes, over, over again.